EASY-TO-LEARN
ENGLISH GRAMMAR
AND PUNCTUATION

PART 1 OF 2

. . .

A STEP-BY-STEP GUIDE FOR A
STRONG ENGLISH FOUNDATION

SITARA MARUF

SuccessTime **Publications**

ISBN: 1499160909
ISBN 13: 9781499160901
Library of Congress Control Number: 2014907155
CreateSpace Independent Publishing Platform
North Charleston, South Carolina

For permission or information, please write or e-mail to Success Time, P.O. Box 83596, Gaithersburg, MD 20883-3596, USA

E-mail: info@successtime.co
           info@learngrammar.net

Phone number: 1-888-331-7486

_____

This book is available for purchase also through these websites.

www.amazon.com   www.amazon.co.uk
www.successtime.co   www.learngrammar.net

Printed in the United States of America.

Find out what is wrong with this sentence and learn a lot more in this easy to use
guide to English grammar and punctuation! (The answer is on page 189.)

EASY-TO-LEARN
ENGLISH
GRAMMAR
AND PUNCTUATION

PART 1 OF 2

· · ·

A STEP-BY-STEP GUIDE FOR A
STRONG ENGLISH FOUNDATION

Parts of Speech, Articles, Capitalization, Punctuation, Double Negatives, Homonyms, and More

 SuccessTime Publications

SITARA MARUF

Table of Contents

PARTS OF SPEECH AND ARTICLES

CAPITALIZATION, CONTRACTIONS, AND PUNCTUATION

Acknowledgments

My heartfelt thanks are due to the following people: my husband and children, who supported my efforts while writing this book and offered suggestions; my parents, especially my late father, for sacrifices that gave the best education to my brothers, sister, and me; my editor Jennifer Razee, for offering the most helpful insights, sound editorial advice, and for making this book the best it could be; the book's cover designer Brian Smith and interior designer Kerrie Robertson, for their creativity, great skills, and contribution to the book's design; the wonderful staff at Logo Design Pros, for their eager collaboration and beautiful artwork with the logo and website development related to this book and delightful contribution to the book's cover; all my teachers, professors, colleagues, and writer friends from the fields of science, journalism, and English, who taught me to think and write clearly and whose contribution to my success is invaluable; all my students, whose honesty, hard work, intellectual curiosity, and appreciation and praise for my teaching methods prompted me to write this book; my friends, for their encouragement, understanding, knowledge, and wisdom—and for being there for me; and I thank all my well-wishers and readers for their support and kindness.

PARTS OF SPEECH
AND ARTICLES

1. Nouns

What is a **noun**?
A noun is a name of a person, place, thing, idea, or quality.

Proper Nouns

A **proper noun** names a specific person, place, animal, or thing. Always begin a proper noun with a capital letter.

Proper Nouns			
Person's name	**Place's name**	**Animal's name**	**Thing's name**
Adam	America	Laika	Taj Mahal
Tina	India	Willy	February
Mary	Washington DC	Daisy	Google
Sania	Niagara Falls	Rocky	American Airlines
Professor Kumar	Hollywood	Lucky	Facebook
Dr. Smith	Pacific Ocean	Toby	Olympics

Common Nouns

A **common noun** names a common person, place, animal, or thing within a group or category. Do not begin a common noun with a capital letter, except when it is the first word in a sentence.

Common Nouns					
Person	**Place**	**Animal**	**Thing**	**Idea**	**Quality**
father	country	dog	rose	independence	honesty
teacher	river	fish	apple	belief	truthfulness
woman	city	lion	chair	center	kindness
doctor	stadium	whale	airplane	goal	sympathy
friend	ocean	kitten	traffic	example	love
writer	school	squirrel	flower	pattern	cruelty

Proper or Common Noun?

Rose: The name **rose** is for a type of flower and not a name for one specific flower or rose. Therefore, **rose** is a common noun for a category of flowers. Do not capitalize **rose,** unless it starts a sentence.

Below, the common noun **roses** begins with a capital *R,* because it is the first word in the sentence.

> ▷   **Roses** are beautiful flowers.

In the sentences below, the common nouns **roses** and **rose** do not begin with a capital *R,* because they do not start the sentence.

> ▷   I bought a bunch of **roses** today.
> ▷   That vase has a yellow **rose**.

Similarly, names of other fruits, vegetables, plants, and trees are common nouns; for example, **mango, apple, pineapple, strawberry, tomato, spinach, lettuce, oak, maple, mulberry**.

Rose (a woman's name): If a woman's name is **Rose**, then it is a proper noun. Always begin with a capital *R,* because it is a name given to a particular woman.

> ▷   I met my friend **Rose** at the library.

doctor: The word **doctor** is a common noun, because it names a group of people in a type of profession.

> ▷   He has an appointment with the **doctor** today.

Dr. Smith is a proper noun, because it is used as a title for a specific doctor.

> ▷   He has an appointment with **Dr. Smith** today.

Count and Noncount Nouns

A count noun can be counted and also has a plural form:
phone/phones,   chair/chairs,   plate/plates,   book/books

A noncount noun cannot be counted, and so it does not have a plural form.

Common Noncount Nouns

Food and drink: rice, salt, tea, coffee, flour, water, ice cream, meat, milk, oil, butter, bread
Material and substances: fabric, wool, iron, wood, gold, furniture, jewelry, bedding

Mass nouns: rain, snow, weather, traffic, mud, sand, sky, air, sunlight, nature, wealth
Abstract nouns: time, knowledge, truth, love, honesty, gravity, energy, wisdom, happiness, freedom, fear, hatred, strength, cowardice, focus, information, pollution

The plural form of noncount nouns refers to the different types in that noun.

Can we write the plural form of **sugar** as **sugars**?

When we say **sugar**, it means one type of **sugar**, which is a noncount noun, and it cannot be written in a plural form. Sometimes we see the word **sugars** on packages and in food and health articles. These **sugars** are the different **types of sugar** in the product.
Do not use the article **a** or **an** before noncount nouns.

- ▷ **Wrong:**   You will get <u>an information</u> tomorrow.
- ▷ **Right:**   You will get <u>the information</u> tomorrow.

- ▷ **Wrong:**   She is looking at <u>a rain</u>.
- ▷ **Right:**   She is looking at <u>the rain</u>.

Noncount nouns are never plural.

- ▷ **Wrong:**   She got new <u>homeworks </u>today.
- ▷ **Right:**   She got new <u>homework </u>today.

- ▷ **Wrong:**   I have <u>eight furnitures</u> in my house.
- ▷ **Right:**   I have <u>some furniture</u> in my house.

Concrete, Abstract, Mass, Collective, and Compound Nouns

Common nouns can be divided into five different types of nouns:

1. Concrete nouns
2. Abstract nouns
3. Collective nouns
4. Mass nouns
5. Compound nouns

1. Concrete nouns are things we can see, touch, taste, hear, or smell.

ribbon, river, mountain, microphone, tree, street, book, television, bus, spoon, dress, window

> **2. Abstract nouns** point to feelings or qualities. We cannot see, touch, taste, or smell abstract nouns.

time, happiness, idea, truth, courage, focus, gravity, love, freedom, honesty, freshness, hatred, wisdom, energy, fear, mercy, greed, selfishness, strength, cowardice, mystery

Abstract nouns are also abstract mass nouns, because they cannot be counted.

> **3. Mass nouns** name things, ideas, or qualities that cannot be counted.

sugar, air, butter, smoke, rain, space, knowledge, water, flour, nature, light, electricity

> **4. Collective nouns** name a whole group or collection of people, animals, or things.

bunch, class, family, orchestra, nation, crowd, committee, traffic, flock, team, herd, batch

> **5. Compound nouns** are made up of two words.

blackboard, train station, sunrise, classroom, ice cream, great-grandmother, caregiver, Indian–American, ringmaster

Example Sentences

1. Tina is a woman.   → Tina = proper noun; woman = common noun
2. February is a month.   → February = proper noun; month = common noun
3. Mary has a great idea.   → Mary = proper noun; idea = common noun
4. Our family is going on vacation.   → family, vacation = common nouns
5. I need some sugar to make tea.   → sugar, tea = common nouns
6. Did you read the newspaper?   → newspaper = common noun

Singular and Plural Nouns

Singular means *one*. Plural means *more than one* or *many*.

Singular nouns (one)	**Plural nouns (more than one)**
one teacher	→ two teachers
one class	→ three classes
one man	→ four men
one child	→ ten children

one woman   two women.

Only count nouns can be made into plural nouns, using the seven rules below.

1. Add **s** to a singular noun.

Singular ↓	table	friend	dog	writer	car
Plural	tables	friends	dogs	writers	cars

2. Add **s** to nouns that end in a vowel **+ y.**

Singular ↓	tray	toy	key	guy	bay	replay
Plural	trays	toys	keys	guys	bays	replays

3. Add **s** to some nouns that end in **f** or **fe.**

Singular ↓	cliff	belief	safe	whiff	puff
Plural	cliffs	beliefs	safes	whiffs	puffs

4. For some other nouns that end in **f** or **fe**, change the **f** to **v** and add **es.**

Singular ↓	scarf	life	knife	wife	leaf
Plural	scarves	lives	knives	wives	leaves

5. Add **es** to singular nouns that end in **s, x, z, ch,** or **sh.**

Singular ↓	dress	box	buzz	watch	sandwich	brush
Plural	dresses	boxes	buzzes	watches	sandwiches	brushes

6. Change the **y** to **i** and add **es** to nouns that end in consonant **+ y.**

Singular ↓	berry	city	country	dictionary	party
Plural	berries	cities	countries	dictionaries	parties

7. **Special plural nouns.** These irregular nouns do not follow any rule but change their spelling when they are made plural.

Singular ↓	child	man	woman	crisis	mother-in-law
Plural	children	men	women	crises	mothers-in-law

8. Some nouns are both singular and plural.

Singular		series	deer	sheep	bison	fish
Plural	↓	series	deer	sheep	bison	fish (one type)
						fishes (different types)

A. **Singular nouns:** The spelling of these nouns ends in **s**, but they are singular.
news, physics, gymnastics, statistics, economics

- ▹ The <u>news is</u> at 6:00 p.m.
  - ○ <u>news</u> = singular noun
  - ○ <u>is</u> = singular verb form

- ▹ <u>Physics is</u> an interesting subject.
  - ○ <u>physics</u> = singular noun
  - ○ <u>is</u> = singular verb form

B. **Plural nouns only:** pants, scissors, glasses

- ▹ Your black <u>pants are</u> in the suitcase.
  - ○ <u>pants</u> = plural noun
  - ○ <u>are</u> = plural verb form

- ▹ Where <u>are</u> my <u>scissors</u>?
  - ○ <u>scissors</u> = plural noun
  - ○ <u>are</u> = plural verb form

How Are Nouns Used in a Sentence?

A noun can be a subject in a sentence.

Most of the time, a sentence has a subject, which is a person, animal, thing, or an idea. So a subject is either a pronoun, a proper noun, or a common noun that is singular or plural. To find out the subject of a sentence, ask *who or what* the sentence is about. If you don't see the subject, the subject may be hidden but easily understood.

- ▹ <u>Katrina</u> is twelve years old.
- ▹ Who is the sentence about? <u>Katrina</u> = proper noun

- ▹ <u>John</u> and <u>Mary</u> are walking along the lake.
- ▹ Who is the sentence about? <u>John and Mary</u> = proper nouns

- ▹ Where are my <u>keys</u>?
- ▹ What is the sentence about? <u>Keys</u> = common noun, plural

- ▹ The <u>bowls</u> and <u>plates</u> are in the cabinet.
- ▹ What is the sentence about? <u>Bowls and plates</u> = common nouns, plural

- ▹ <u>Freedom</u> is every person's birthright.
- ▹ What is the sentence about? <u>Freedom</u> = common noun, abstract

A noun can be a subject complement (predicate noun) in a sentence.

The subject complement describes the subject and comes after the linking verbs **to be**, **to appear, to seem, to become, to remain**, and so on. When the subject is linked to a noun, it is called a predicate noun. A sentence with a predicate noun can be reversed.

- ▹ Natasha is the highest-scoring student.
    - ○ <u>Natasha</u> = subject
    - ○ predicate noun = <u>student</u>

When we reverse the sentence, the predicate noun switches with the subject.

- ▹ The highest-scoring student is Natasha.
    - ○ <u>student</u> = subject
    - ○ predicate noun = <u>Natasha</u>

- ▹ Next year Ms. Jones will be the principal.
    - ○ <u>Ms. Jones</u> = subject
    - ○ predicate noun = <u>principal</u>

- ▹ Next year the principal will be Ms. Jones.
    - ○ <u>principal</u> = subject
    - ○ predicate noun = <u>Ms. Jones</u>

- ▹ The man in the white coat appears to be the doctor.
    - ○ <u>man</u> = subject
    - ○ predicate noun = <u>doctor</u>

- ▹ The doctor appears to be the man in the white coat.
    - ○ <u>doctor</u> = subject
    - ○ predicate noun = <u>man</u>

A noun can be a direct object in a sentence.

The direct object is a person, animal, thing, or an idea that receives the action of the verb. Ask the questions *whom* or *what* in relation to the subject and verb.

> ⟩ Adam kicked the ball.
>   - ○ Adam = subject
>   - ○ kicked = verb
>   - ○ ball = direct object (common noun)

What action did Adam do? Kicked the ball. Ball receives the action of the verb kicked.

> ⟩ Seema likes her science teachers.
>   - ○ Seema = subject
>   - ○ likes = verb
>   - ○ teachers = direct object (common noun)

Whom does Seema like? Her science teachers. The object teachers receives the action of the verb likes.

> • From my window I saw a rainbow.
>   - ○ I = subject
>   - ○ saw = verb
>   - ○ rainbow = direct object (common noun)

What is the action? Seeing a rainbow. Rainbow receives the action of the verb saw.

> • I will speak only the truth.
>   - ○ I = subject
>   - ○ speak = verb
>   - ○ truth = direct object (abstract noun)

What is the action? Speaking the truth. Truth receives the action of the verb speak.

A noun can be an indirect object in a sentence.

An indirect object is a person, animal, thing, or an idea that *indirectly* receives the action of the verb. The indirect object is usually written between the subject and the direct object. To find the indirect object, ask the questions *to whom* or *for whom* is the work being done.

> ⟩ Sharon gave her brother a coat.
>   - ○ Sharon = subject
>   - ○ gave = verb

What did Sharon give? A coat. (coat = direct object, common noun)
To whom did Sharon give? To her brother. (brother = indirect object, common noun)

> ⟡ Tina is lending <u>Mary</u> some money.
>   ○ <u>Tina</u>= subject
>   ○ <u>is lending</u> = verb

What is Tina lending? Some money. (<u>money</u> = direct object, common noun)
To whom is Tina lending? To Mary. (<u>Mary</u> = indirect object, proper noun)

> ⟡ May I show <u>Mr. Smith</u> my article?
>   ○ <u>I</u> = subject
>   ○ <u>show</u> = verb

What may I show Mr. Smith? My article. (<u>article</u> = direct object, common noun)
To whom do I want to show? Mr. Smith. (<u>Mr. Smith</u> = indirect object, proper noun)

A noun can be an object complement.

Sometimes, the direct object needs another noun, pronoun, or an adjective to complete its meaning. These words or phrases are called object complements, and they always follow the direct object.

> ⟡ My sister calls me <u>Bubbly</u>.
>   ○ <u>me</u> = direct object
>   ○ <u>Bubbly</u> = object complement

The noun <u>Bubbly</u> is needed to complete the meaning of the direct object <u>me</u> and also the meaning of the sentence.

> ⟡ The committee has made her <u>president</u>.
>   ○ her = direct object
>   ○ president = object complement

The noun <u>president</u> is needed to complete the meaning of the direct object <u>her</u> and also the meaning of the sentence.

A noun can show possession or ownership.

A possessive noun tells who owns what. To show possession with singular nouns, just add an apostrophe and *s* to the noun.

Examples

1. Sania's car
2. John's desk
3. Adam's aunt
4. Tina's house

When a singular noun ends with **s**, follow the above general rule of adding an apostrophe and **s.**

Examples

Charles' lecture	→ **okay**
Charles's lecture	→ **better**
Jesus' teachings	→ **okay**
Jesus's teachings	→ **better**

To show possession with plural nouns, add only an apostrophe after the plural form.

Ownership with singular nouns (one person, one thing)	**Ownership with plural nouns (more than one person, more than one thing)**
one <u>teacher**'s**</u> book	→ two <u>teacher**s'**</u> books
one <u>class**'s**</u> exam	→ two <u>class**es'**</u> exams
one <u>man**'s**</u> computer	→ two <u>men**'s**</u> computers
one <u>child**'s**</u> blanket	→ two <u>children**'s**</u> blankets

If two or more people own the same thing, only the last noun is possessive.

Examples:

1. Tim and Sameer's house (one house)
2. Neil and Seema's mother (one mother)

If two or more people own different things, each noun is possessive.

Examples:

1. Rihanna's and Meena's cars (two different cars)
2. Anthony's and Tina's computers (two different computers)

A noun can be an object of the preposition.

> We played during the <u>recess</u>.
>   ○ <u>during</u> = preposition
>   ○ <u>recess</u> = common noun that is an object of the preposition <u>during</u>
>   ○ <u>We</u> = subject
>   ○ <u>played</u> = verb

- ▹ The soap bottle is under the <u>sink</u>.
  - ○ <u>under</u> = preposition
  - ○ <u>sink</u> = common noun that is an object of the preposition <u>under</u>
  - ○ <u>soap bottle</u> = subject
  - ○ <u>is</u> = verb

- ▹ You will work until the <u>weekend</u>.
  - ○ <u>until</u> = preposition
  - ○ <u>weekend</u> = common noun that is an object of the preposition <u>until</u>
  - ○ <u>You</u> = subject
  - ○ <u>will work</u> = verb

A noun can be an appositive.

An appositive is a noun or noun phrase that renames a noun or pronoun, which may be a subject or an object. The appositive may also explain or give information about the noun or pronoun. If the appositive is needed to complete the meaning of the sentence, do not use a comma. If the appositive is used only to give additional information, separate the appositive with a comma.

- ▹ Mumbai, <u>a city in India</u>, has the largest film industry, popularly known as Bollywood.

The appositive <u>a city in India</u> renames the subject, <u>Mumbai</u>.
The appositive is not needed for the sentence, as the meaning of the sentence would be complete without the appositive. Therefore, the appositive is separated by commas.

- ▹ The underwater photographers <u>Anthony Jones and Akbar Tabb</u> won awards for best photography.

The appositive <u>Anthony Jones and Akbar Tabb</u> renames the <u>subject</u>, the two <u>photographers.</u>
The names <u>Anthony Jones and Akbar Tabb</u> are needed to know which underwater photographers won the awards. Therefore, there are no commas around the appositive.

- ▹ We are visiting Pompeii, <u>the ancient Roman city</u>.

The appositive <u>the ancient Roman city</u> renames the object, <u>Pompeii</u>, and is not necessary to the meaning of the main clause (<u>We are visiting Pompeii</u>), so it is separated by a comma.

- ▹ Please send your questions to our volunteers, <u>the main workers of this project</u>.

The appositive <u>the main workers of this project</u> renames the object, <u>volunteers,</u> and is not necessary to the meaning of the main clause ("<u>Please send your questions to our volunteers</u>"), so it is separated by a comma.

Nouns and Gender

Sometimes a noun changes for a male or female person or animal. Other times, a noun may not change at all, and we use the common or neuter gender for such nouns. Accordingly, nouns have four genders.

Nouns that refer to a person or animal have masculine and feminine forms; however, nouns that had masculine and feminine forms to refer to people in professions or jobs, do not use the feminine nouns anymore. In modern usage, the masculine noun in professions and jobs is used as a common gender noun for both males and females.

1. **Masculine gender** refers to a male person or animal. Examples: man, boy, uncle, king, dog, lion.

2. **Feminine gender** refers to a female person or animal. Examples: woman, girl, auntie, queen, bitch, lioness.

3. **Common gender** refers to some person or animal which is male or female. In the past, nouns belonging to professions or jobs were masculine and feminine; but nowadays, the masculine nouns have been accepted as common nouns for male and female persons.

Examples of professions or jobs: doctor, engineer, servant, astronaut, leader, nurse, flight attendant, author, actor, teacher

Examples of other common nouns: child, cousin, neighbor, friend, enemy

Common gender nouns and nouns of some animals can be made into their masculine and feminine forms by adding a modifier such as **male, female, he**, or **she**.

Masculine—Feminine
1. male teacher—female teacher
2. male doctor—female doctor / lady doctor
3. male giraffe—female giraffe

4. **Neuter gender** refers to things that are not male or female. Examples: paper, pen, rock, tree, mountain, house, computer, cloud, chair, room.

Examples of Masculine and Feminine Gender Nouns

Masculine—Feminine
actor—actress (The use of *actress* is old-fashioned but sometimes needed to describe the female character in the movie or play.)
brother—sister
duke—duchess
emperor—empress
gentleman—lady
heir—heiress

hero—heroine
host—hostess
hunter—huntress
husband—wife
king—queen
landlord—landlady
man—woman
monk—nun
nephew—niece
prince—princess
sir—madam
son—daughter
uncle—aunt
waiter—waitress
widower—widow
wizard—witch

Some Animal Nouns

General Noun	Masculine	Feminine	Baby animals
cat	tomcat	cat	kitten
cattle	bull / ox	cow	calf
deer	buck	doe	fawn
donkey	jack	jenny	foal
duck	drake	duck	duckling
goose	gander	goose	gosling
horse	stallion	mare	foal (colt=male; filly=female)
pig	boar	sow	piglet
sheep	ram	ewe	lamb
bee	drone	queen	
	cock /rooster	hen	chick
	dog	bitch	puppy
	lion	lioness	cub
	tiger	tigress	cub, whelp
	fox	vixen	cub, kit, pup

(For more discussion on nouns, please see *Easy-to-Learn English Grammar and Punctuation, Part 2 of 2.*)

■ ■ ■

Noun Exercises

> **1A.** Write **proper** or **common** next to each noun.
> Also write if the noun is abstract, collective, or compound where appropriate.

	Noun	Noun type		Noun	Noun type
Examples:	1. Shalimar	proper		2. group	common (collective)
1.	England	_____	8.	wisdom	_____
2.	Himalaya	_____	9.	kindness	_____
3.	singer	_____	10.	airport	_____
4.	company	_____	11.	band	_____
5.	China	_____	12.	Washington	_____
6.	bus depot	_____	13.	Sheraton	_____
7.	sister	_____	14.	English	_____

> **1B.** Underline the nouns in the sentences and write the word(s) under *Proper* or *Common*.

Sentences	Proper	Common
Example: _February_ is a _month._	February	month
1. India is a country.		
2. People speak different languages.		
3. My friend, Adam, knows the truth.		
4. The Taj Mahal is beautiful.		
5. We must work for peace.		
6. We must have patience all the time.		
7. The sun gives us light and heat.		
8. The Nile River is long.		
9. Our team won the game.		
10. The Pacific Ocean is the largest ocean.		

> **1C.** Write *abstract* or *concrete* in front of the nouns below.

Noun	Type	Noun	Type
Examples: 1. loyalty	abstract	2. cake	concrete
1. traffic	_____	6. calculator	_____
2. window	_____	7. honesty	_____
3. happiness	_____	8. truth	_____
4. grief	_____	9. coffee	_____
5. jungle	_____	10. head	_____

1D. Please put an apostrophe where needed to indicate possession.

Example 1: The passengers ticket is lost. = The <u>passenger's</u> ticket is lost.
Example 2: The childrens mother went to the clinic. = The <u>children's</u> mother went to the clinic.

1. The boys money is on the desk.

   _____

2. The dancers costumes are beautiful. (two answers)

   _____

3. Indias population is over one billion.

   _____

4. The girls racquets are in the locker. (two answers)

   _____

5. My mothers purse is brown.

   _____

■ ■ ■

2. Pronouns

Like a noun, a pronoun names a specific person or thing.
Many times a pronoun stands in place of a noun.

The first sentence below uses only nouns. The second sentence uses nouns and pronouns.

> ▷ Sharon is helping Sharon's brother with the brother's math homework.
> ▷ Sharon is helping **her** brother with **his** math homework.

The pronoun **her** is in place of Sharon.
The pronoun **his** is in place of the brother.

Types of Pronouns

1. Personal
2. Interrogative
3. Demonstrative
4. Relative
5. Intensive
6. Reflexive
7. Indefinite

Singular	Personal Pronouns			Intensive and reflexive pronouns
	Subject pronouns	Object pronouns	Possessive pronouns	
1. First person (speaker)	I	me	my, mine	myself
2. Second person (listener)	you	you	your, yours	yourself
3. Third person (who is being talked about)—masculine	he	him	his	himself
4. Third person—feminine	she	her	her, hers	herself
5. Third person—neutral	it	it	its	itself
Plural				
6. First person—Others and I	we	us	our, ours	ourselves
7. Second person—Many listeners	you	you	your, yours	yourselves
8. Third person—people, things, animals, places, and so on.	they	them	their, theirs	themselves

Subject Pronouns

I, You, He, She, It, We, They

Subject pronouns are used as subjects of a sentence. The sentence is about them, which means subject pronouns do whatever a noun can do.

Singular subjects	Singular subject pronouns
1. <u>I</u> (the speaker)	▷ <u>I</u> am working at the computer.
2. <u>You</u> (the listener)	▷ <u>You</u> are playing with the dog.
3. <u>The man</u> is going to work.	▷ <u>He</u> is going to work.
4. <u>The woman</u> is reading a book.	▷ <u>She</u> is reading a book.
5. The <u>bird</u> is sitting on the roof.	▷ <u>It</u> is sitting on the roof.
Plural subjects	**Plural subject pronouns**
6. <u>My mother</u> and <u>I</u> are going to the movie.	▷ <u>We</u> are going to the movie.
7. <u>Sunny and Tina, you</u> are not studying. (two or more listeners)	▷ <u>You</u> are not studying.
8. <u>The students</u> are quiet.	▷ <u>They</u> are quiet.

The pronouns **I, you,** and **we** are used by both males or females.
He is always masculine and is used for a boy or man.
She is always feminine and is used for a girl or woman.
You can be used for talking to one person or more than one person. Also, "**you are**" is used in singular and plural forms.

Example Sentences

> ▷ Seema, **you** are enjoying today.
> ▷ Neil and Nikki, **you** are enjoying today.

They can be used for more than one person, animal, or thing.

> ▷ The birds are flying. = **They** are flying.
> ▷ Mary, Adam, and Mini are walking. = **They** are walking.

It is a neutral gender and can be used for an animal, thing, place, idea, or feeling. Sometimes **it** is used only as a subject to talk in a general way. In these situations **it** does not stand in for any noun or nouns.

In the examples below, **it** is used only as a subject and not to replace nouns:

> ▷ **It** is raining.
> ▷ **It** feels wonderful to hear from you.
> ▷ How does **it** feel to be in a new country?

- ▷ **It** is a great idea!
- ▷ Is **it** okay to sit down?
- ▷ **It** gets hot in the room after some time.
- ▷ **It** is a fact that some people live for more than one hundred years.
- ▷ **It** bothers me that I have to explain every time.

In the examples below, **it** is used as a subject to replace nouns:

- ▷ **The job** is difficult. = **It** is difficult.
- ▷ **The place** is beautiful. = **It** is beautiful.
- ▷ **The bird** came out of its cage. = **It** came out of its cage.
- ▷ **The tree** fell down. = **It** fell down.

Subject pronouns function as subjects of a sentence. There may be more than one subject in the sentence, and you may need to use more than one subject pronoun.

- ▷ **She** and **I** cleaned the office.
  - ○ She and I = subject pronouns
  - ○ cleaned = action (common verb for both subjects)

- ▷ **He** said that **they** will go with the children.
  - ○ He and they = subject pronouns
  - ○ verb for he = said
  - ○ verb for they = will go

Object Pronouns

Me, You, Her, Him, It, Us, Them

Object pronouns are used as objects in a sentence. Object pronouns show the receiver of the action.

Singular object	Singular object pronouns
1. Tina, you give the book to **me**.	▷ You give the book to **me**.
2. Mary, I will send an e-mail to **you**.	▷ I will send an e-mail to **you**.
3. We will give a present to that **girl**.	▷ We will give a present to **her**.
4. They will talk to the **boy**.	▷ They will talk to **him**.
5. [You] Do not hit the **chair**.	▷ [You] Do not hit **it**.
Plural objects	**Plural object pronouns**
6. I am calling a taxi for **my brother and me**.	▷ I am calling a taxi for **us**.
7. They will explain the matter **to you and everyone** here.	▷ They will explain the matter to **you**.
8. I will send chocolates **to Sharon, Sunny, and Tina**.	▷ I will send chocolates to **them**.

Object pronouns function as direct objects of verb (action), indirect objects of verb (action), and objects of prepositions. An object pronoun is the receiver of action. In a sentence there may be more than one receiver of action, and you may need to use more than one object pronoun. The action receivers (object pronouns) will not have a verb, because they are not the doer of action.

Object Pronoun as Object of a Preposition

- ▷ Adam threw the ball to **him.**
  - ○ <u>Adam</u> = subject
  - ○ <u>threw</u> = verb (action)
  - ○ **him** = object pronoun, the receiver of action
  - ○ <u>to</u> = preposition
  - ○ <u>to him</u> = prepositional phrase

- ▷ The scientist explained to **them**.
  - ○ <u>scientist</u> = subject
  - ○ <u>explained</u> = verb (action)
  - ○ **them** = object pronoun is the receiver of action
  - ○ <u>to</u> = preposition
  - ○ <u>to them</u> = prepositional phrase

- ▷ They were inquiring about **us**.
  - ○ subject pronoun = <u>they</u>
  - ○ <u>were inquiring</u> = verb (action)
  - ○ **us** = object pronoun, the receiver of action
  - ○ <u>about</u> = preposition
  - ○ <u>about us</u> = prepositional phrase

Object Pronoun as Direct Object of a Verb

- ▷ My aunt scolded **me**.
  - ○ <u>aunt</u> = subject
  - ○ <u>scolded</u> = verb
  - ○ **me** = object pronoun, the receiver of action

- ▷ We invited **them**.
  - ○ <u>we</u> = subject
  - ○ <u>invited</u> = verb
  - ○ **them** = object pronoun, the receiver of action

Object Pronoun as Indirect Object of a Verb

- ▷ [You] Please show **her** the class notes.
  - ○ The subject **you** is understood.
  - ○ <u>show</u> = verb

- ○ **her** = object pronoun is the receiver of action (indirect object)
- ○ <u>class notes</u> = direct object

> He must tell **them** about our situation.
>   - ○ <u>He</u> = subject pronoun
>   - ○ <u>tell</u> = verb
>   - ○ **them** = object pronoun is the receiver of action (direct object)
>   - ○ situation = object of preposition
>   - ○ <u>about</u> = preposition
>   - ○ <u>about our situation</u> = prepositional phrase

Possessive Pronouns

**My, Your, His, Her, Its, Our, Your, Their /
Mine, Yours, His, Hers, Ours, Yours, Theirs**

Possessive pronouns show ownership or possession. Unlike nouns, possessive pronouns do not use the apostrophe. There are two kinds of possessive pronouns:

1. Possessive Pronouns as Limiting Adjectives: **My, Your, His, Her, Its, Our, Your, Their**
2. Independent Possessive Pronouns: **Mine, Yours, His, Hers, Ours, Yours, Theirs**

Possessive Pronouns as Limiting Adjectives: My, Your, His, Her, Its, Our, Your, Their
These possessive pronouns come before a noun, and they function as adjectives to qualify nouns. These pronouns cannot stand alone in a sentence, and they always need an object.

> Where is **my** card?
>   - ○ my = possessive pronoun as an adjective
>   - ○ card = noun (object)

> This is **their** typewriter.
>   - ○ their = possessive pronoun as an adjective
>   - ○ typewriter = noun (object)

> Exception: The pronoun **<u>his</u>** can be used as an adjective as well as an independent possessive pronoun.

> He likes **his** presents.
>   - ○ **his** = possessive pronoun as an adjective
>   - ○ presents = noun (object)

> He likes **his**.
>   - ○ **his** = independent possessive pronoun

> Those are **his** shoes.
>> ○ **his** = possessive pronoun as an adjective
>> ○ shoes = noun (object)

> Those are **his**.
>> ○ **his** = independent possessive pronoun

Independent Possessive Pronouns: Mine, Yours, His, Hers, Ours, Yours, Theirs
These pronouns can stand alone in a sentence and do not need a definite object. They do not function as limiting adjectives; but they replace nouns, so they can be treated as nouns.

Four Uses of Independent Possessive Pronouns:

1. A replacement for one or more possessive nouns.

> This seat is Natasha's. = This seat is **hers.**
> Those towels are Adam's and John's. = Those towels are **theirs.**

2. Subject of a verb.

> Your ice cream melted quickly.= **Yours** melted quickly.
> Our bus will arrive soon = **Ours** will arrive soon.
> Her headband is on the counter. = **Hers** is on the counter.

3. Object of a verb.

> Share your chocolates. = Share **yours.**
> Take our dinnerware. = Take **ours.**
> Clean his car. = Clean **his**.

(**His** can be used as an adjective and an independent pronoun.)

5. Object of a preposition.

> Add my contribution to **hers.**
> Take these bags with **theirs.**
> She is a friend of **mine**.

<u>Possessive Pronouns as Limiting Adjectives</u>	<u>Independent Possessive Pronouns</u>
(A noun follows the possessive pronoun.)	(The noun is replaced by these possessive pronouns.)
> Where are **my** keys?	> Where are **mine**?
> Remember to take **your** umbrella.	> Remember to take **yours**.

- ▹ That is **his** computer.
- ▹ Look at **her** purse.
- ▹ The bird flew from **its** nest.
- ▹ Please bring **our** sweaters.
- ▹ Put new batteries in **your** cameras.
- ▹ They forgot to take **their** photos.

- ▹ That computer is **his**.
- ▹ Look at **hers**.
- ▹ The nest is **its**.
- ▹ Please bring **ours**.
- ▹ Put new batteries in **yours**.
- ▹ They forgot to take **theirs**.

A possessive pronoun has the same gender as the noun it replaces.	
John's book = **his** book (John is a boy, so we say **his** book.)	Reena's book = **her** book (Reena is a girl, so we say **her** book).
Adam's sister = **his** sister (Adam is a boy, so we say **his** sister.)	Sheeba's sister = **her** sister (Sheeba is a girl, so we say **her** sister.)
The dog's tail = **Its** tail	The car's lights = **Its** lights
Neal and Tim's mother = **their** mother mother of two boys = **their** mother	Seema and Reena's mother = **their** mother mother of two girls = **their** mother.

The possessive form of the noun has an apostrophe: **Reena's** teacher, **Adam and Tim's** car, the **dog's** tail, the **car's** lights.

The possessive form of the pronoun does not have an apostrophe: **her** teacher, **their** car, **its** tail, **its** lights.

Note the difference between the contraction *it's* and possessive pronoun *its*	
Its = One-word **possessive pronoun.** No apostrophe.	**It's** = It is or It has (two words) The apostrophe in **it's** shows that the letter *i* is missing from **it is**, and the letters *ha* are missing from **it has.**
▹ The **phone's** battery is dead. = **Its** battery is dead. ▹ The **bottle's** lid is dirty. = **Its** lid is dirty.	▹ **It is** a crowded place. = **It's** a crowded place. ▹ **It has** been a difficult time = **It's** been a difficult time.

Interrogative Pronouns

What, Who, Whom, Which, Whose

An interrogative pronoun is used to ask a question. *To interrogate* means to *ask.*
These are interrogative pronouns:

- ▹ **Who** is going to come for dinner?
- ▹ **Whom** did you see yesterday?

> **Which** movie is good?
> **What** is the matter?
> **Whose** book did you borrow?

Demonstrative Pronouns

This, That, These, Those

The demonstrative pronoun is used to show things. *To demonstrate* means to show.

Singular: this, that   (for one person, thing, idea, or place)
Plural: these, those   (for persons, things, ideas, or places)

Example Sentences

> **This** is a thick book. (For one book, which is here.)
> **These** are thick books. (For many books, which are here.)
> **That** is a small classroom. (For one classroom, which is there.)
> **Those** are small classrooms. (For many classrooms, which are there.)

Relative Pronouns

What, When, Where, Who, Whom, Whose, Which, Why, That

Relative pronouns are used to connect two sentences that have the same noun or pronoun.

Compound Relative Pronouns: Whoever, Whomever, Whichever, and Whatever
Relative pronouns also relate groups of words. They do not change with gender or number.

Connecting two sentences with a relative pronoun:

> The person took me to school. The person is my father.
> The person **who** took me to school is my father. (who = relative pronoun)

   In the above sentence, **who** relates to **person**.
   The relative clause is **"who took me to school."**

> I talked to the children this morning. The children seemed happy.
> The children **whom** I talked to this morning seemed happy. (whom = relative pronoun)

> We saw a movie last week. The movie was boring.
> The movie **that** we saw last week was boring. (that = relative pronoun, restrictive or necessary)

> ⊳ The teacher gave the questions. The questions are in the math textbook.
> ⊳ The questions, **which** the teacher gave, are in the math textbook.
> (<u>which</u> = relative pronoun, nonrestrictive, or, not necessary to convey meaning of main clause)

> ⊳ We used to chat for hours in the garden. Do you remember those days?
> ⊳ Do you remember the days **when** we used to chat for hours in the garden?
> (<u>when</u> = relative pronoun)

> ⊳ The stolen items were not found. Only the police know about them.
> ⊳ Only the police know **what** happened to the stolen items. (<u>what</u> = relative pronoun)

> ⊳ These are the steps. We used to sit here during breaks.
> ⊳ These are the steps **where** we used to sit during breaks. (<u>where</u> = relative pronoun)

> ⊳ He did not come to the college reunion. No one knows the reason.
> ⊳ No one knows **why** he did not come to the college reunion. (<u>why</u> = relative pronoun)

> ⊳ I met the child. The child's family is from Indonesia.
> ⊳ I met the child **whose** family is from Indonesia. (<u>whose</u> = relative pronoun)

> ⊳ You have something on your mind. Please say it.
> ⊳ Please say **whatever** you have on your mind. (<u>whatever</u> = relative pronoun)

> ⊳ We have some books. Choose the book that is easy to read.
> ⊳ Choose **whichever** book is easy to read. (<u>whichever</u> = relative pronoun)

Intensive and Reflexive Pronouns

Myself, Yourself, Himself, Herself, Itself, Ourselves, Yourselves, Themselves

Intensive and reflexive pronouns are same, but their uses are different.

Subject pronoun	Intensive and reflexive pronouns
1. I	→ myself
2. You	→ yourself
3. He	→ himself (not hisself)
4. She	→ herself
5. It	→ itself
6. We	→ ourselves
7. You	→ yourselves
8. They	→ themselves (not theirselves)

Intensive pronouns are used to emphasize the subject, which is usually a noun or pronoun. If you remove the intensive pronoun, the meaning of the sentence does not change. Since intensive pronouns do not receive the action of the subject, they are not objects in the sentence.

▷ I **myself** called the police.
The word **myself** is not necessary in the sentence, but it adds emphasis to the pronoun **I**.

▷ You made the arrangements **yourself**.
The word **yourself** is not necessary in the sentence, but it adds emphasis to the pronoun **you**.

▷ My students **themselves** came up with the idea.
The word **themselves** is not necessary in the sentence, but it adds emphasis to the noun **students**.

▷ The dog **itself** chased the cat away.
The word **itself** is not necessary in the sentence, but it adds emphasis to the noun **dog**.

Reflexive Pronouns

Intensive and reflexive pronouns are same, but their uses are different. When the subject and object is the same in the sentence, reflexive pronouns refer back to the subject. A reflexive pronoun comes after the verb and is the object of that verb. So a reflexive pronoun receives the action of the verb.

The reflexive pronoun is always used with its corresponding subject pronoun.
Examples:

I / **myself**; you / **yourself**; he / **himself**; her / **herself**; it / **itself**;
we / **ourselves**; you / **yourselves**; they / **themselves**

Reflexive pronouns function as the following:

▷ **A direct object of the verb (action):**

▷ We entertained **ourselves** while you were at work.
subject verb   reflexive pronoun

▷ John will not defeat **himself** before trying.
subject   verb   reflexive pronoun

▷ **An indirect object of the verb (action):**

▷ I   got **myself** help from the police. (help = direct object; myself =indirect object)
subject   verb reflexive pronoun

⊳   You can reward **yourself** with a vacation.
     subject   verb   reflexive pronoun

     (vacation = direct object; yourself = indirect object)

⊳   **An object of a preposition:**

⊳   The queen sings **to herself.** (to = preposition)
         subject   reflexive pronoun

⊳   You can work **for yourself**. (for = preposition)
     subject   reflexive pronoun

Sometimes the reflexive pronoun comes before the subject and reflects back to the subject (noun or pronoun).

⊳   To entertain **themselves**, they watched a movie.
                  reflexive pronoun   subject

⊳   To protect **himself** from lightning, Neal got inside the building.
                reflexive pronoun   subject

⊳   To clean **yourself**, [you can] use the tap water on the beach.
              reflexive pronoun   subject

     Here, the subject pronoun **you** is understood, and **you** reflects back to the reflexive pronoun **yourself.**

If the subject and object is same, use a reflexive pronoun to reflect back to its subject. Before using a reflexive pronoun, see if it has the corresponding subject pronoun or noun in the sentence, and if it can refer back to its subject. If it does not have the corresponding subject, you may need only a simple subject pronoun (*I, you, he, she, it, we, they*) or object pronoun (*me, you, him, her, it, us, them*).

In the wrong sentences below, the reflexive pronoun **yourself** does not have its corresponding subject pronoun **you.** Therefore, the sentences need only a simple subject and object pronoun **you** and not the reflexive pronoun **yourself**.

Wrong   → We are inviting people like **yourself** to the meeting.
Right   → We are inviting people like **you** to the meeting.
                    ○   **you** = object pronoun

Wrong   → I am doing well—and **yourself**?
Right   → I am doing well—and **you**?
                    ○   **you** = subject pronoun

In the first sentence below, **myself** does not have its corresponding subject pronoun **I.** Therefore, the object pronoun **me** is needed as the object of the verb **invited.**

Wrong	→ The director invited my wife and <u>**myself**</u> to his son's wedding.
Right	→ The director invited my wife and <u>**me**</u> to his son's wedding.
	○ **me** = object pronoun

In the example below, the subject and object is same, therefore, the subject pronoun **I** needs its reflexive pronoun **myself.** The pronoun **myself** reflects back to its corresponding subject pronoun **I**.

Wrong	→ I gave <u>**me**</u> a birthday present.
Right	→ I gave <u>**myself**</u> a birthday present.
	○ **myself** = reflexive pronoun reflects back to its subject pronoun **I**

Indefinite Pronouns

Some pronouns take the place of a noun or refer to nouns in a general manner. They do not point to nouns in a definite or specific way. Therefore, these pronouns are called indefinite pronouns.

Below are some indefinite pronouns listed alphabetically.
all, another, any, anybody, anyone, anything, both, each, either, everybody, everyone, everything, few, little, many, more, most, much, neither, nobody, none, no one, nothing, one, other, others, several, some, somebody, someone, something

The same word can be an indefinite pronoun in one sentence and an adjective in another sentence. So how do you know if that word is an indefinite pronoun or an adjective? There is no noun after an indefinite pronoun, but there is a noun after an adjective. See the sentence pairs below:

> **Some** are still waiting to hear from us.
> (some = indefinite pronoun)

> **Some** people are still waiting to hear from us.
> (**some** = adjective that modifies the noun **people**)

> **Many** are taking part in the sports competition.
> (**many** = indefinite pronoun)

> **Many** students are taking part in the sports competition.
> (**many** = adjective that modifies the noun **students**)

> **Both** attended the school conference.
> (**both** = indefinite pronoun)

> **Both** parents attended the school conference.
> (**both** = adjective that modifies the noun **parents**)

> **Nobody** bothers to clean up after using the tables.
> (**nobody** = indefinite pronoun)

> **Several** books fell down from the shelf.
> (**several** = adjective that modifies the noun **books**)

(For more discussion on pronouns, please see *Easy-to-Learn English Grammar and Punctuation, Part 2 of 2.*)

■ ■ ■

Pronoun Exercises

> **2A.** Use the subject pronouns, **he, she, it, we,** or **they** to match the following.

Example: Monica and I = __we__

1. John and Tina = _they_	2. My parents = _they_	3. Amar = _____
4. Rita = _She_	5. The chair = _It_	6. The boats = _____
7. Sania and friends = _They_	8. My friends, my mother, and I = _we_	
9. The books and pen = _It_	10. Maryam, Natasha, and I = _we_	

> **2B.** Use pronouns below in place of the underlined nouns.

Example. <u>John and Sonia</u> are playing. (__They__)

1. <u>Soniya, Tina, and I</u> will go downstairs. (_we_)
2. <u>Katrina</u> is older than <u>Abraham</u>. (_She_ , _him_)
3. <u>My brother's</u> car is in the repair shop (_His_)
4. <u>Tina's</u> earrings are in the drawer. (_Her_)
5. <u>John and Anthony</u> will go to college. (_They_)
6. <u>Sheeba, Natasha, and I</u> know everything. (_we_)
7. <u>The project's</u> deadline is over. (_Its_)
8. <u>Sania</u> is asking <u>Natasha, Reena, and Neil</u>. (_She_ , _them_)
9. I found <u>the watch</u> by the sink. (_It_)
10. <u>Many ships</u> are sailing in the sea. (_They_)

> **2C.** Change the underlined nouns to pronouns. Rewrite the sentences, and add **to** if needed.

1. I didn't sell Tim my <u>computer</u>. _I didn't see it to him._

2. My sister will babysit the <u>children</u>. _____

3. They are giving us a <u>gift</u>. _They are give it to us ✓_

4. Seema was talking with her <u>uncle</u>. _____

5. We cannot do without <u>money</u>. _____

> **2D.** Are the underlined words reflexive pronouns or intensive pronouns? Write **R** for reflexive and **I** for intensive pronoun.

*Examples: 1. You made those arrangements **yourself**. (I)*
*2. They bought **themselves** sandwiches and tea. (R)*

1. She **herself** can talk to the doctor about **herself.** _____, _____
2. We **ourselves** can entertain **ourselves.** _____, _____
3. Reena **herself** walked to the door and opened it. _____
4. The computer shut **itself** during the storm. _____
5. They could do the show, but they ruined the chance **themselves**. _____
6. I want to kick **myself** for helping the wrong person. _____
7. You can reward **yourself** with a vacation, after you finish that project. _____
8. She **herself** chose to stay home and not come to the movie. _____
9. Sameer told **himself** not to worry about the exam results. _____
10. The door opened by **itself**. _____
11. We must congratulate **ourselves** for preparing well. _____
12. Mary sings to **herself**. _____
13. Hooray! I did it **myself**. _____
14. She is looking at **herself** in the mirror. _____
15. My sister caught the thief **herself**. _____
16. The road **itself** is very dangerous. _____
17. They should not complain, when they **themselves** wanted to walk in the hot afternoon. ____
18. We want to handle this **ourselves**. _____
19. Allow Maya to talk to David **herself**. _____
20. The printer will not start **itself** after a power failure. _____

> **2E.** Underline the correct pronoun.
> In some sentences both pronouns may be correct.

*Example 1: The school principal is **she / her**.*
*Example 2: She **herself / himself** chose to stay home and not come to the movie.*

1. They found the thief **who / whom** stole your wallet.
2. I saw an old friend **that / whose** name I had forgotten.
3. **Our / ours** class is in the evening.
4. Many people told **us / we** not to bring our computers.
5. **These / this** tomatoes are better than **them / those**.

6. The chocolates **that / which** you want are in the kitchen.
7. We cannot sleep because **yourself /you** snore too much.
8. I will share my lunch with **whoever / whomever** wants to share with me.
9. They will do **their / theirs** work. We will do **our/ours**.
10. A cousin **whom / who** I never met is coming to our house today.
11. If we go too far, **our / your** parents will worry.
12. She enjoyed our dinner, and said thanks to **us /me**.
13. Send it to **whoever / whomever** needs it now.
14. **Neither / someone** has been smiling a lot today.
15. **Whom / Who** should we contact for the job?
16. **No one / many** enters through that door.
17. Is **your / mine** uncle going to **their / they** wedding?
18. I like **this / these** blanket better than **that / those**.
19. The gift bags are **theirs / their.**
20. The chair is broken. **Its / it** legs were weak.
21. I don't know **who / whom** you are talking about.
22. **She / they** has to do her homework herself.
23. I gave **me / myself** a birthday present.
24. We will buy from **whomever / whoever** you suggest.
25. **Both / some** of my brothers are doctors.
26. **Most / few** students are in class today.
27. Give me **whichever / whatever** ticket is available.
28. **Most / any** of the house is clean.
29. The hard-working students are Mary and **I / myself**.
30. The prizewinners, Sameer and **him / she**, were requested to give a speech.

2F. Rewrite the sentences using the correct pronoun.

Example: (We, Us, Them) walked with (they, her, he) to her home.
   _We_ *walked with **her** to her home.*

1. (She, Her, Hers) and (me, I) had a fight.

   _____

2. (You, Yours, Your) and (her, hers, she) will work tomorrow.

   _____

3. (Us, We, Them) had invited (they, him, she) to meet with the students.

   _____

4.   Those dirty clothes are (him, she, hers).

_____

5.   The teacher wrote to (them, we, they).

_____

6.   Are you going to eat (these, this) chips?

_____

7.   (We, Us, Me) asked for directions, but no one knew.

_____

8.   The manager told two workers and (me, she, they) not to bring food.

_____

9.   (Hers, Her, She) and (me, I) have not met for many days.

_____

10. (These, This) eggs are rotten.

_____

2G. Use subject pronouns**, I, you, he, she, it, we,** or **they,** for the underlined words.

Example: <u>My brother and sister</u> are playing.   *They*

I am John. I work in a bank. My parents' names are Anthony and Mary. 1) <u>My parents</u> live with us. I have two children. 2) In the morning, <u>my children and I</u> leave home at the same time. I go by car. 3) <u>My children</u> go to school by bus. My wife is from India. 4) <u>My wife</u> speaks three languages. 5) <u>My children, my wife, and I</u> will visit India soon. My father reads the newspaper in the morning. 6) <u>My father</u> has good knowledge. My mother loves to cook and teach. 7.) <u>My mother</u> also loves to go for walks. 8) <u>My parents, my wife, my children, and I</u> have dinner together.

■ ■ ■

3. Verbs

A verb is a word that shows action, work, state, or condition of someone or something. Verbs give life to sentences. Sometimes only one verb is enough to make a meaningful sentence:
Help! Run!   Drink!
In the above examples, the subject is *you* (the listener).

Verbs express action and work:
  ‣ I <u>sang</u> till eleven o'clock last night.
  ‣ You <u>go</u> to school now.
  ‣ He <u>washed</u> all the clothes yesterday.
  ‣ She <u>drives</u> to her office every day.
  ‣ It <u>finished</u> all the milk this morning.

Verbs express a condition or state:
  ‣ We <u>are worried</u> about our exam results.
  ‣ They <u>were happy</u> to see you.
  ‣ The dress <u>looks</u> lovely.
  ‣ The computer <u>has</u> a virus.

Action verbs: An action verb shows action that can be seen or heard, such as **speak, write, shout, dance, carry, push, eat, run,** and **fall.** Action verbs also show action that cannot be seen or heard, such as **breathe, think, hear, smell, wonder, dream, grow, sleep, understand,** and **worry.** So action verbs express physical action as well as quiet and slow actions.

Verb tenses: A verb tense shows whether the action happened in the past, is happening in the present, or will happen in the future.
The English language has twelve kinds of verb tenses, as shown by the example on page 71. In this book, however, we will study six of them in detail. Please see Part 2 to learn about the other six verb tenses.

Let's begin with the six tenses of the common verbs **to be, to have,** and **to do.**

Six Tenses of *Be*

1. Simple present tense	2. Simple past tense	3. Simple future tense
▹ I <u>am</u>. ▹ You/we/they <u>are</u>. ▹ He/she/it <u>is</u>.	▹ I /he/she/it <u>was</u>. ▹ You/we/they <u>were</u>.	▹ I/you/he/she/it/we/they <u>will be</u>.
4. Present progressive or present continuous	**5. Past progressive or past continuous**	**6. Future progressive or future continuous**
▹ I <u>am being</u>. ▹ You/we/they <u>are being</u>. ▹ He/she/it <u>is being</u>.	▹ I /he/she/it <u>was being</u>. ▹ You/we/they <u>were being</u>.	▹ I/you will/he/she/it/we/they <u>will be being</u>.

❖ **1 Simple Present Tense of *Be***

The simple present tense shows an action, habit, state, or situation that is happening now or happens regularly. The present tense is also used to show a fact or general beliefs and actions.

The present tense of <u>be</u> has three words: <u>am</u>, <u>is</u>, and <u>are</u>.
   ▹ I <u>am</u>.
   ▹ You / we / they <u>are</u>.
   ▹ He / she / it <u>is</u>.

> <u>Am</u>, <u>is</u>, and <u>are</u> are the main verbs in the present tense of <u>be</u>.

<u>Singular (one)</u>	<u>Plural (more than one)</u>
1. I <u>am</u> a girl.	1. We <u>are</u> girls.
2. You <u>are</u> a boy.	2. You <u>are</u> boys.
3. She <u>is</u> a teacher.	3. They <u>are</u> teachers.
4. He <u>is</u> a doctor.	4. They <u>are</u> doctors.
5. It <u>is</u> a pen.	5. They <u>are</u> pens.

❖ **2 Simple Past Tense of *Be***

The simple past tense shows that an action or state has been completed before now.
The past tense of <u>be</u> has two words: <u>was</u> and <u>were</u>.
   ▹ I/he/ she/it <u>was</u>.
   ▹ You / we / they <u>were</u>.

> Was and were are the main verbs in the past tense of be.

Singular (one)	Plural (more than one)
1. I was a child in 1980.	1. We were children in 1980.
2. You were a baby in 1985.	2. You were babies in 1985.
3. He was in school few years ago.	3. They were in school few years ago.
4. She was at home today.	4. They were at home today.
5. It was a puppy five years ago.	5. They were puppies five years ago.

❖ 3 Simple Future Tense of *Be*

The simple future tense shows that an action will take place in the future.
Future tense = will + be

The future-tense form will be remains the same for all pronouns and nouns, whether they are singular or plural.

⊳   I/you/he/she/it/we/they will be.

> Will is the helping verb, and be is the main verb, in the future tense of be.

Singular (one)	Plural (more than one)
1. I will be a doctor in few years.	1. We will be doctors in few years.
2. You will be happy.	2. You will be happy.
3. He will be going to school next year.	3. They will be going to school next year.
4. She will be living in England soon.	4. They will be living in England soon.
5. It will be a great vacation.	5. They will be great vacations.

❖ 4 The Present Progressive or Present Continuous Tense of *Be*

The present progressive tense shows action that is continuing now. Most of the time, the action lasts for a short time.

Present progressive tense of be = present tense of be + ing form of be (present participle)

1) am + being;   2) is + being;   3) are + being

Use the *-ing* form of the main verb to make all progressive tenses. The *-ing* form is also called the present participle. It shows that the action is continuing for some time around the present. However, we cannot use only the present participle (being) as a verb. To make the present continuous tense of be, use being with the present tense of be (am/ is/ are) as helping verbs.

- ▷ I being nice.   **Wrong**
- ▷ I am being nice.   **Correct**

Be is the only verb that can be a helping verb and a main verb in the same sentence!
In the present continuous tense of be, the helping verb (am / is / are) and the main verb (being) comes from be.

- ▷ I am being nice.
- ▷ You/we/they are being nice.
- ▷ He/she/it is being nice.

> Am, is, and are are helping verbs and present-tense forms of be. The main verb is being.

Singular (one)	Plural (more than one)
1. I am being nice every day.	1. We are being nice every day.
2. You are being silly today.	2. You are being silly today.
3. He is being nasty this week.	3. They are being nasty this week.
4. She is being helpful.	4. They are being helpful.
5. It is being naughty.	5. They are being naughty.

Use be as a helping verb to show the present progressive tense of another verb.

Example: to play
Present progressive tense of play = present tense of be + playing (present participle)

1) am + playing;   2) is + playing;   3) are + playing

We cannot use only the present participle (playing) as a verb. To make the present continuous tense of play, use playing with the present tense of be (am, is, and are) as helping verbs.

- ▷ I playing.   **Wrong**
- ▷ I am playing.   **Correct**

Be is the helping verb (am, is, and are) for present participles of other verbs too!

- ▷ I am playing.
- ▷ You/we/they are playing.
- ▷ He/she/it is playing.

Am, is, and are are helping verbs and the present-tense forms of be.
The main verbs below are playing, going, teaching, talking, and swimming.

Singular (one)	Plural (more than one)
1. I am playing now.	1. We are playing now.
2. You are going to school.	2. You are going to school.
3. She is teaching.	3. They are teaching.
4. He is talking.	4. They are talking.
5. It is swimming.	5. They are swimming.

❖ 5 The Past Progressive or Past Continuous Tense of *Be*

The past progressive tense shows action or condition that was continuing in the past and has been completed.

Past progressive tense of be = past tense of be + ing form of be (present participle)

1) was + being   2) were + being

Was and were show that the action was completed in the past. Being shows that the action was continuous for some time. To make the past continuous tense of be, use the *-ing* form of be (being) with the past tense of be (was and were) as helping verbs.

> ▹ You being nice yesterday.   **Wrong**
> ▹ You were being nice yesterday.   **Correct**

In the past continuous tense of be, the helping verb (was / were) and the main verb (being) comes from be.

> ▹ I /he/she/it was being.
> ▹ You/we/they were being.

Was and were are helping verbs and the past-tense forms of be. The main verb is being.

Singular (one)	Plural (more than one)
1. I was being nice on our last picnic.	1. We were being nice on our last picnic.
2. You were being silly yesterday.	2. You were being silly yesterday.
3. He was being nasty in the meeting.	3. They were being nasty in the meeting.
4. She was being helpful.	4. They were being helpful.
5. It was being naughty while you were out	5. They were being naughty while you were out.

Be as a helping verb to show the past progressive tense of another verb.
Example: to play

Past progressive tense = past tense of be + ing form of main verb
1) was + playing   2) were + playing

We cannot use only the present participle (playing) as a verb. To make the past continuous tense of play, use playing with the past tense of be (was /were) as helping verbs.

‣	I playing in the morning.	**Wrong**
‣	I/he/she/it was playing.	**Correct**
‣	You/we/they were playing.	**Correct**

> In the examples below, was and were are helping verbs and past-tense forms of be. The main verbs are playing, going, teaching, talking, and swimming.

1. I was playing in the morning.
2. You were going to school at 9:00 a.m.
3. She was teaching.
4. He was talking.
5. It was swimming.

1. We were playing in the morning.
2. You were going to school at 9:00 a.m.
3. They were teaching.
4. They were talking.
5. They were swimming.

❖ **6 The Future Progressive or Future Continuous Tense of *Be***

The future progressive tense shows continuing action or a condition that will happen in the future.

Future progressive tense of be = future tense of be + ing form of be
= will + be + being
be = helping verb; being = main verb
> Will I be being a clown at Anita's birthday party?

Be as a helping verb shows the future progressive tense of another verb.
Example: to play

Future progressive tense = will + be + ing form of play
will + be + playing

We cannot use only the present participle (playing) as a verb. To make the future continuous tense of play, use playing with the helping verbs will and be.
> I playing next month.   **Wrong**
> I will be playing next month.   **Correct**

The helping verbs <u>will be</u> remain the same for all pronouns and nouns, whether they are singular or plural.

> ▷   I/he/she/it/ you/we/they <u>will be playing</u>.

<u>Will be</u> are helping verbs. The main verbs below are <u>playing, going, teaching, talking</u>, and <u>swimming</u>.

1. I <u>will be playing</u> next month.
2. You <u>will be going</u> to school tomorrow.
3. She <u>will be teaching</u> in the afternoon.
4. He <u>will be talking</u>.
5. It <u>will be swimming</u>.

1. We <u>will be playing</u> next month.
2. You <u>will be going</u> to school tomorrow.
3. They <u>will be teaching</u> in the afternoon.
4. They <u>will be talking</u>.
5. They <u>will be swimming</u>.

Six Tenses of *Have*

1. Simple present tense	2. Simple past tense	3. Simple future tense
▷ I/you/we/they <u>have</u>. ▷ He/she/it <u>has</u>.	▷ I/you/he/she/it/we/ they <u>had</u>.	▷ I/you/he/she/it/we/they <u>will have</u>.
4. Present progressive or present continuous	**5. Past progressive or past continuous**	**6. Future progressive or future continuous**
▷ I/you/we/they <u>are having</u>. ▷ He/she/it <u>is having</u>.	▷ I /you/he/she/ it /we/ they <u>were having</u>.	▷ I/you/he/she/it/we/they <u>will be having</u>.

❖ **1 Simple Present Tense of *Have***

The present tense of <u>have</u> has two forms: <u>have</u> and <u>has</u>.

> ▷   I /you/we/they <u>have</u>.
> ▷   He / she / it <u>has</u>.

<u>Have</u> and <u>has</u> are main verbs in the sentences below.

Singular (one)	Plural (more than one)
1. I <u>have</u> three phones today.	1. We <u>have</u> three phones today.
2. You <u>have</u> a car.	2. You <u>have</u> a car. / You <u>have</u> cars.
3. She <u>has</u> a new job now.	3. They <u>have</u> new jobs now.
4. He <u>has</u> a computer.	4. They <u>have</u> a computer. / They <u>have</u> computers.
5. It <u>has</u> a garage.	5. They <u>have</u> a garage. / They <u>have</u> garages.

❖ 2 Simple Past Tense of *Have*

The past tense of the verb <u>have</u> is <u>had</u> for all pronouns and nouns, whether they are singular or plural.

    ⊳   I/you/ he/ she/it / we / they <u>had</u>.

> <u>Had</u> is the main verb in the past tenses below.

Singular (one)	Plural (more than one)
1. I <u>had</u> three phones yesterday.	1. We <u>had</u> three phones yesterday.
2. You <u>had</u> a car last week.	2. You <u>had</u> a car last week. / You <u>had</u> cars last week.
3. She <u>had</u> a new job recently.	3. They <u>had</u> new jobs recently.
4. He <u>had</u> three computers.	4. They <u>had</u> a computer. / They <u>had</u> three computers.
5. It <u>had</u> a garage.	5. They <u>had</u> a garage. / They <u>had</u> garages.

❖ 3 Simple Future Tense of *Have*

The future tense of <u>have</u> is <u>will have</u> for all pronouns and nouns, whether they are singular or plural.

    ⊳   I/you/he/she/it/we/they <u>will have</u>.

> <u>Will</u> is the helping verb and <u>have</u> is the main verb in the future tenses below.

Singular (one)	Plural (more than one)
1. I <u>will have</u> three phones soon.	1. We <u>will have</u> three phones soon.
2. You <u>will have</u> a car in a month.	2. You <u>will have</u> a car in a month. / You <u>will have</u> cars in a month.
3. She <u>will have</u> a new job.	3. They <u>will have</u> new jobs.
4. He <u>will have</u> a computer.	4. They <u>will have</u> a computer. / They <u>will have</u> computers.
5. It <u>will have</u> a garage.	5. They <u>will have</u> a garage. / They <u>will have</u> garages.

❖ **4 The Present Progressive or Present Continuous Tense of** *Have*

Present progressive tense = present tense of <u>be</u> + <u>having</u> (present participle)
am / is / are + having

> ▹ I <u>am having</u>.
> ▹ He / she / it <u>is having</u>.
> ▹ You/ we/ they <u>are having</u>.

Have or having?

<u>Having</u>, which makes up the progressive tense of <u>have</u>, is used only to show an experience, an event, and certain actions, such as eating or drinking, that have a short time period. For many other states that do not show continuous changes in physical actions, the present-tense verb <u>have</u> is used.

> ▹ I am having a headache.   **Wrong**
> ▹ I <u>have</u> a headache.   **Correct**
>
> ▹ We are having a student named David.   **Wrong**
> ▹ We <u>have</u> a student named David.   **Correct**
>
> ▹ The house is having an air-conditioner.   **Wrong**
> ▹ The house <u>has</u> an air-conditioner.   **Correct**
>
> ▹ I am having a chemistry exam next week.   **Wrong**
> ▹ I <u>have</u> a chemistry exam next week.   **Correct**

In the present progressive tenses below, <u>am</u>, <u>is</u>, and <u>are</u> are helping verbs, and <u>having</u> is the present participle and main verb.

Singular (one)	Plural (more than one)
1. I <u>am having</u> an omelet.	1. We <u>are having</u> omelets.
2. You <u>are having</u> a party.	2. You <u>are having</u> a party.
3. She <u>is having</u> difficulty learning this.	3. They <u>are having</u> difficulty learning this.
4. He <u>is having</u> fun.	4. They <u>are having</u> fun.
5. It <u>is having</u> a good time.	5. They <u>are having</u> a good time.

❖ **5 The Past Progressive or Past Continuous Tense of** *Have*

Past progressive tense = past tense of <u>be</u> + <u>having</u> (present participle)
was / were + having

> ▹ I <u>was having</u>
> ▹ He /she /it <u>was having</u>
> ▹ You/ we/ they <u>were having</u>

> In the past progressive tense below, <u>was</u> and <u>were</u> are helping verbs. <u>Having</u> is the present participle and main verb.

Singular (one)	Plural (more than one)
1. I <u>was having</u> an omelet when you knocked.	1. We <u>were having</u> omelets when you knocked.
2. You <u>were having</u> a party.	2. You <u>were having</u> a party.
3. She <u>was having</u> difficulty learning this.	3. They <u>were having</u> difficulty learning this.
4. He <u>was having</u> fun yesterday.	4. They <u>were having</u> fun yesterday.
5. It <u>was having</u> a good time.	5. They <u>were having</u> a good time.

❖ **6 The Future Progressive or Future Continuous Tense of *Have***

Future progressive tense = future tense of <u>be</u> + <u>having</u> (present participle)

I/you/he/she/it/we/they <u>will be having</u>.

The future progressive tense of <u>have</u> has one form for all pronouns and nouns, whether they are singular or plural: <u>will be having</u>.

> <u>Will be</u> are helping verbs, and <u>having</u> is the present participle and main verb in the future progressive tense below.

Singular (one)	Plural (more than one)
1. I <u>will be having</u> a party soon.	1. We <u>will be having</u> a party soon.
2. You <u>will be having</u> a good time.	2. You <u>will be having</u> a good time.
3. She <u>will be having</u> a baby soon.	3. They <u>will be having</u> a baby soon.
4. He <u>will be having</u> fun next week.	4. They <u>will be having</u> fun next week.
5. It <u>will be having</u> a bad experience.	5. They <u>will be having</u> a bad experience.

Six Tenses of *Do*

1. Simple present tense	2. Simple past tense	3. Simple future tense
▷ I/you/we/they <u>do</u>. ▷ He/she/it <u>does</u>.	▷ I/you/he/she/it/we/they <u>did</u>.	▷ I/you/he/she/it/we/they <u>will do</u>.
4. Present progressive or present continuous	**5. Past progressive or past continuous**	**6. Future progressive or future continuous**
▷ I/you/we/they <u>are doing</u> ▷ He/she/it <u>is doing</u>	▷ I/you/he/she/it/we/they <u>were doing</u>	▷ I/you/he/she/it/we/they <u>will be doing</u>

❖ 1 Simple Present Tense of *Do*

The present tense of <u>do</u> has two forms: <u>do</u> and <u>does</u>.

> ▷ I /you/we/they do.
> ▷ He / she / it does.

> <u>Do</u> and <u>does</u> are main verbs in the present tense below.

Singular (one)	Plural (more than one)
1. I <u>do</u> my homework every day.	1. We <u>do</u> our homework every day.
2. You <u>do</u> the dishes.	2. You <u>do</u> the dishes.
3. She <u>does</u> the cooking from 4:00 to 6:00 p.m.	3. They <u>do</u> the cooking from 4:00 to 6:00 p.m.
4. He <u>does</u> exercises in the morning.	4. They <u>do</u> exercises in the morning.
5. It <u>does</u> a great job.	5. They <u>do</u> a great job.

❖ 2 Simple Past Tense of *Do*

The past tense of <u>do</u> has one form: <u>did.</u>
> ▷ I /you/ he / she / it /we/they <u>did</u>.

> In the past tense examples below, <u>did</u> is the main verb:

Singular (one)	Plural (more than one)
1. I <u>did</u> my homework yesterday.	1. We <u>did</u> our homework yesterday.
2. You <u>did</u> the dishes last Saturday.	2. You <u>did</u> the dishes last Saturday.
3. She <u>did</u> the cooking by 6:00 p.m.	3. They <u>did</u> the cooking by 6:00 p.m.
4. He <u>did</u> exercises every day.	4. They <u>did</u> exercises every day.
5. It <u>did</u> a great job.	5. They <u>did</u> a great job.

❖ 3 Simple Future Tense of *Do*

The future tense of <u>**do**</u> has one form for all pronouns and nouns, whether they are singular or plural: <u>**will do**</u>.

> ▷ I /you/he/she/it/we/they <u>will do.</u>

> Do is the main verb, and will is the helping verb in the past tense below.

Singular (one)	Plural (more than one)
1. I will do my homework later.	1. We will do our homework later.
2. You will do the dishes this Saturday.	2. You will do the dishes this Saturday.
3. She will do the cooking at 4:00 p.m.	3. They will do the cooking at 4:00 p.m.
4. He will do exercises every day.	4. They will do exercises every day.
5. It will do a great job.	5. They will do a great job.

❖ **4 The Present Progressive or Present Continuous Tense of *Do***

Present progressive tense = present tense of be + doing (present participle)

Be as a helping verb (am/ is/ are) is illustrated below:

- ➢   I am doing
- ➢   He / she / it is doing
- ➢   You/ we/ they are doing

> Doing is the main verb, and am, is, and are are helping verbs in the present tense below.

Singular (one)	Plural (more than one)
1. I am doing interviews now.	1. We are doing interviews now.
2. You are doing nothing.	2. You are doing nothing.
3. She is doing a good job this year.	3. They are doing a good job this year.
4. He is doing research.	4. They are doing research.
5. It is doing well.	5. They are doing well.

❖ **5 The Past Progressive or Past Continuous Tense of *Do***

Past progressive tense = past tense of be + doing (present participle)

Be as a helping verb (was / were) is illustrated below:

- ➢   I / he / she / it was doing
- ➢   You/ we/ they were doing

> Doing is the main verb, and was and were are helping verbs in the past progressive tense below.

Singular (one)	Plural (more than one)
1. I was doing interviews for three hours.	1. We were doing interviews for three hours.
2. You were doing nothing today.	2. You were doing nothing today.
3. She was doing a good job last year.	3. They were doing a good job last year.
4. He was doing research recently.	4. They were doing research recently.
5. It was doing well.	5. They were doing well.

❖ 6 The Future Progressive or Future Continuous Tense of *Do*

The future progressive tense of do has one form for all pronouns and nouns, whether they are singular or plural: will + be + doing.

Future progressive tense = will + be + doing

> ⊳ I /you/ he / she / it/we /they will be doing

Doing is the main verb, and will be are helping verbs in the future progressive tense below.

Singular (one)	Plural (more than one)
1. I will be doing interviews between 3:00 and 5:00 p.m. tomorrow.	1. We will be doing interviews between 3:00 and 5:00 p.m. tomorrow.
2. You will be doing nothing when I am away.	2. You will be doing nothing when I am away.
3. She will be doing a good job.	3. They will be doing a good job.
4. He will be doing research.	4. They will be doing research.
5. It will be doing well.	5. They will be doing well.

Transitive and Intransitive Verbs

Action verbs are divided into two groups: transitive verbs and intransitive verbs.

> ⊳ Transitive: Natasha buys a magazine every week. (magazine = direct object)
> ⊳ Intransitive: Natasha buys every week.

> ⊳ Transitive: I am writing a speech. (speech = direct object)
> ⊳ Intransitive: I am writing.

> ⊳ Transitive: She understands your problem. (problem = direct object)
> ⊳ Intransitive: She understands.

Transitive verbs always have a direct object. Ask the question, "What object is there for the subject to complete its action?" Also ask the question, "Whom?" If you find the answer, the verb in the sentence is transitive.

- ⊳   Tina **closed** the door.
  - ○   What did Tina close? The door. (<u>door</u> = direct object)

- ⊳   I **saw** many children today.
  - ○   Whom did I see? Children. (<u>children</u> = direct object)

- ⊳   She **ate** a sandwich for lunch.
  - ○   What did she eat? A sandwich. (<u>sandwich</u> = direct object)

Intransitive verbs do not have a direct object, but they show the subject's action or movement. A prepositional phrase may follow the intransitive verb.

Below, the prepositional phrases are underlined, and the intransitive verb is boldface.
Note that there is no object.

- ⊳   I **am going** <u>to the hospital.</u>
- ⊳   He just **laughed.**
- ⊳   They **were talking** <u>about the robbery.</u>

Linking Verbs

A linking verb describes the nature, personality, character, or state of the subject. It links a subject (noun or pronoun) to an adjective, a noun, or an adverb that describes the subject. It can also link a subject (noun or pronoun) to an adjective phrase, a noun phrase, or an adverb phrase. The linking verb does not have a direct object.

- ⊳   <u>Reena</u> **is** smart. (Linking verb <u>is</u> links <u>Reena</u> to the adjective <u>smart</u>.)
- ⊳   <u>Reena</u> **became** a doctor. (Linking verb <u>became</u> links <u>Reena</u> to the noun <u>doctor</u>.)
- ⊳   <u>Reena</u> **was** in London. (Linking verb <u>was</u> links <u>Reena</u> to the adverb of place <u>London</u>.)

Linking verbs from <u>be</u>: am, is, are, was, were, am being, is being, was being, were being, can be, could be, may be, may have been, might be, might have been, must be, shall be

Other common linking verbs: appear, look, seem, feel, taste, sound, smell, become, keep, remain, stay, get, go, grow, turn

Linking verb followed by an adjective or adjective phrase that describes the subject:

- ⊳   Today the teacher <u>appears</u> angry.
- ⊳   You <u>sound</u> very good on YouTube.
- ⊳   The scene <u>turned</u> pleasant in few minutes.

Linking verb followed by a noun, noun phrase, or pronoun that renames the subject:

- ▷ She <u>became</u> a great writer.
- ▷ It <u>is</u> she. ("It is her" is acceptable in casual conversations.)
- ▷ He <u>sounded</u> like a chief executive of the company.
- ▷ It <u>appears</u> to be a plane.

Linking verb followed by an adverb or adverb phrase:

- ▷ The class <u>is</u> at 9:00 a.m.
- ▷ They <u>appeared</u> quietly.
- ▷ My house <u>is</u> on Second Street.
- ▷ The party <u>was</u> then; the meeting <u>is</u> now.

Helping or Auxiliary Verbs

Helping verbs help the main verb give some idea of the time of action to show the present, past, or future tense. Helping verbs are always written before the main verb, and together they are called a verb phrase. A verb phrase may have a main verb and up to three helping verbs. If the sentence has the word <u>not</u>, it is usually between the helping verb and the main verb.

Note the twenty-three helping verbs:

- • is, am, are, was, were, be, being, been   (from the verb <u>be</u>)
- • has, have, had   (from the verb <u>have</u>)
- • do, does, did   (from the verb <u>do</u>)
- • will, shall, should, would
- • can, could
- • may, might, must

Sentences	Helping verbs	Main verb
1. Tim <u>was selling</u> his car to buy a new one.	was	selling
2. He <u>should have been</u> happy to hear the news.	should have	been
3. I <u>will be calling</u> you tomorrow.	will be	calling
4. Mom is happy that I <u>will be</u> home in summer.	will	be
5. We <u>are going</u> to meet the boss.	are	going
6. <u>Did</u> you not <u>show</u> them the budget?	did	show
7. <u>Have</u> you <u>worked</u> on a similar project before?	have	worked
8. John <u>is being</u> nasty today.	is	being

Basic Verb

The basic verb form (*play, look*) is found in the dictionary and also called the bare infinitive. The basic form does not change with number or gender, but it needs a helping verb. The same basic form is used for all nouns and pronouns.

Examples:

1. play
2. look
3. arrive
4. bake

In the sentences below, the basic verbs are underlined and boldface; the helping verbs are underlined.

- ⯈   I/you/he/she/it/we/they/ someone/everyone <u>can</u> **<u>play.</u>**
- ⯈   I/you/he/she/it/we/they/ someone/everyone <u>must</u> **look** for the exit door.
- ⯈   I/you/he/she/it/we/they/ someone/everyone <u>may</u> **arrive** soon.
- ⯈   I/you/he/she/it/we/they/ someone/everyone <u>will</u> **bake** the chicken.

Infinitive

When you add <u>to</u> to the basic verb, (*to play, to look*) it becomes an infinitive, which is the root of the verb. The infinitive does not change with number or gender, as other verbs do, and the sentence can never be complete with the infinitive verb alone. The infinitive can be used as a verb, noun, adjective, or an adverb with another functioning verb.

Examples:

1. to play
2. to look
3. to arrive
4. to bake

In the sentences below, the infinitives are underlined and boldface, whereas the main verbs are underlined. Note that the infinitive remains the same for all persons, tenses, mood, and gender, but the main verb changes according to the persons, tense, and mood.

- ⯈   I **<u>to play</u>** tennis.   **Wrong**
- ⯈   I / you /we/ they <u>want</u> **<u>to play</u>** tennis.   **Correct**
- ⯈   She/ he /someone /everyone <u>wants</u> **<u>to play</u>** tennis.   **Correct**
      (<u>want /wants</u> = verb; <u>to play</u> = infinitive)

⊳	You **to look** at the screen.		**Wrong**
⊳	You <u>have</u> **to look** at the screen		**Correct**
	(<u>have</u> = verb; <u>to look</u> = infinitive)		

⊳	She **to take** the class tomorrow.		**Wrong**
⊳	She <u>decided</u> **to take** the class tomorrow.		**Correct**
	(<u>decided</u> = verb; <u>to take</u> = infinitive)		

⊳	We **to reach** today.		**Wrong**
⊳	We <u>are going</u> **to reach** today.		**Correct**
	(<u>are going</u> = verb; <u>to reach</u> = infinitive)		

⊳	They **to work** next week.		**Wrong**
⊳	They <u>will come</u> **to work** next week.		**Correct**

Regular Verbs

Regular verbs follow the same pattern when the tenses are changed. Regular verbs change into their past tense or past participle by adding **ed** or **d** to the basic form. However, when the basic forms end in **p, b, m,** or **g,** add **-ped, -bed, -med,** and **–ged** respectively.

Examples of Regular Verbs

Basic form			Past tense	Past participle		Present participle
1. arrive	+ d →		arrived	arrived	arriv + ing →	arriving
2. bake	+ d →		baked	baked	bak + ing →	baking
3. play	+ ed →		played	played	play + ing →	playing
4. look	+ ed →		looked	looked	look + ing →	looking
5. clip	+ ped →		clipped	clipped	clip + ping →	clipping
6. rub	+ bed →		rubbed	rubbed	rub + bing →	rubbing
7. trim	+ med →		trimmed	trimmed	trim + ming →	trimming
8. hug	+ ged →		hugged	hugged	hug + ging →	hugging

Please refer to the chart of regular verbs on page 64-66.

Irregular Verbs

Note—Irregular verbs follow the same rule as regular verbs to form simple present and future tenses but follow an irregular pattern to form their past tense and past participle.

Like regular verbs, an irregular verb does not form its past tense and past participle by adding **d** or **ed.** In fact, irregular verbs do not follow any regular pattern to form their past tense. Their past tense and past participle forms are very different from the basic verb. The only way to know the past tense and past participle forms of irregular verbs is to learn them.

Examples of Irregular Verbs

Basic form	Past tense	Past participle	Present participle
1. go	went	gone	going
2. break	broke	broken	breaking
3. see	saw	seen	seeing
4. sit	sat	sat	sitting
5. cut	cut	cut	cutting

We use the verbs to be, to do, and to have many times daily. These verbs are irregular, and they function as helping verbs as well as main verbs, depending on the sentence. Note that their verb forms are very different from the basic parent verb.

The verbs forms of <u>be</u>: 1) am 2) is 3) are 4) was 5) were 6) be 7) being 8) been
The verbs forms of <u>have</u>: 1) have 2) has 3) had 4) having
The verbs forms of <u>do</u>: 1) do 2) does 3) did 4) doing 5) done

Helping verbs are used in the same way with irregular verbs as they are used with regular verbs.

Simple Present Tense

We have learned the tenses of the common verbs <u>be</u>, <u>have</u>, and <u>do</u>. Here, we will study six tenses of regular and irregular verbs.

As we know, the simple present tense shows an action, habit, state, or situation that is happening now or happens regularly. The present tense is also used to show a fact or general beliefs and actions.

Example: <u>help</u> = regular verb

> ⚬ I / you / we / they <u>help</u> every day. (<u>help</u> = basic form)
> ⚬ He / she / it / someone / everyone <u>helps</u> every day. (<u>helps</u> = basic form + <u>s</u>)

The simple present tense has two types of forms:
The basic form (**work, clean**) for *I, you, we,* and *they*
The basic form + **s** (**works, cleans**) for *he, she,* and *it*

Note—The indefinite pronouns, such as <u>someone, everyone, somebody, everybody,</u> and <u>nobody,</u> are third-person singular and take singular verbs (**works, cleans**)

work, works;   play, plays;   clean, cleans;   write, writes;   come, comes.

If the verb ends in **s, x, o, ch, sh,** and **zz,** add **es** to the third-person singular. If the verb ends in one **z,** add **zes.**

<u>Verb</u>	<u>Sentences in third-person singular</u>
1. guess + es:	He <u>guesses</u> the answer.
2. discuss + es:	Tanya <u>discusses</u> with us. (<u>Tanya</u> = she)
3. catch + es:	It <u>catches</u> insects.
4. match + es:	The color <u>matches</u> perfectly. (<u>color</u> = it)
5. brush + es:	He <u>brushes</u> his teeth twice.
6. finish + es:	She <u>finishes</u> the work quickly.
7. mix + es:	Mary <u>mixes</u> the flour, eggs, and butter for the cake. (<u>Mary</u> = she)
8. relax + es:	Our dog <u>relaxes</u> on the sofa.
9. quiz + zes:	She <u>quizzes</u> us on all test topics.
10. whiz + zes:	The bee <u>whizzes</u> around me every now and then. (<u>bee</u> = it)
11. buzz +es:	That woman <u>buzzes</u> about with all kinds of rumors. (<u>woman</u> =she)
12. go + es:	He <u>goes</u> to the beach when it is sunny and hot.
13. do + es:	She <u>does</u> the makeup for the actors.
14. try = change *y* to *ies*:	It <u>tries</u> very hard to climb the wall.
15. fly = change *y* to *ies*:	Adam <u>flies</u> big passenger planes. (<u>Adam</u> =he)

Note—Irregular verbs follow the same rule as regular verbs to form simple present and future tenses but follow an irregular pattern to form their past tense.

Examples with irregular verbs: <u>sit, drive, come,</u> and <u>go</u>

> I/you/ we/they <u>sit</u> in the office every day. (<u>sit</u>= basic form)
> He/she/it/someone/everyone <u>sits</u> in the office every day. (<u>sits</u> = basic form + <u>s</u>)

> I/you/we/they <u>drive</u> to New York tomorrow.
> He/she/someone/everyone <u>drives</u> to New York tomorrow.

> I/you/we/they <u>come</u> to the library often.
> She/he/it /someone/everyone <u>comes</u> to the library often.

> I/you/we/they <u>go</u> to school.
> She/he/it /someone/everyone <u>goes</u> to the library often.

Uses of the Present Tense

> **The present tense shows regular action:**
> I /you/we/they <u>work</u> every day.
> He/she/it <u>works</u> every day.
> Someone/everyone <u>works</u> every day.
> I/you/we/they <u>relax</u> in the evenings.
> He/she/it <u>relaxes</u> in the evenings.
> Someone/everyone <u>relaxes</u> in the evenings.

> **The present tense shows a current state or situation:**
> She <u>seems</u> busy.
> They <u>appear</u> confident.
> Here <u>comes</u> our friend. (<u>friend</u> = third-person singular)
> There <u>goes</u> our money. (<u>money</u> = third-person singular)

<u>Be</u> is the only verb whose present tense is different from its basic form, <u>be</u>. The present tenses of <u>be</u> are <u>am</u>, <u>is</u>, and <u>are</u>.

> I <u>am</u> tired.
> She /he/it/someone/everyone <u>is</u> thirsty.
> You/we/they <u>are</u> happy.

> **The present tense shows a situation or condition that happens often:**
> The lines <u>are</u> always long in the evenings. (<u>lines</u> = third-person plural, basic form = <u>be</u>)
> Our office <u>is</u> closed on weekends. (<u>office</u> = third-person singular, basic form = <u>be</u>)
> Many countries <u>have</u> a visa requirement. (<u>countries</u> = third-person plural, basic form = have)
> The building <u>has</u> a security camera. (<u>building</u> = third-person singular, basic form = <u>have</u>)

> **The present tense shows an action at a scheduled time:**
> I <u>start</u> next week.
> You <u>teach</u> on Wednesday.
> He <u>joins</u> next month.
> She <u>arrives</u> on May 29 at 5:00 p.m.
> It <u>reopens</u> tomorrow.
> We <u>send</u> mail every other day.
> They <u>close</u> this Sunday.
> The strike <u>ends</u> tomorrow.   (<u>strike</u> = noun = third person singular)
> The schools <u>reopen</u> tomorrow.   (<u>schools</u> = noun = third person plural)

You can also use the future tense for some of the above sentences.

> I will <u>start</u> next week.
> She will <u>arrive</u> on May 29 at 5:00 p.m.
> Schools will <u>reopen</u> tomorrow.
> I/you/we/they/ he/ she/someone/everyone <u>will</u> drive to New York tomorrow.

> **The present tense shows a well-known fact:**
> The earth <u>has</u> one moon. (<u>earth</u> = <u>it</u> = third-person singular)
> Usually, germs <u>get</u> in through our noses and mouths. (<u>germs</u> = they = third-person plural)
> Water <u>is</u> necessary for life. (<u>water</u> = <u>it</u> = third-person singular)
> The new date <u>begins</u> at midnight. (<u>date</u> = <u>it</u> = third-person singular)

> **The present tense shows a common saying or belief:**
> [You] <u>Look</u> before you <u>leap</u>. (The first <u>you</u> is understood. <u>You</u> = second-person singular and plural.)
> Many hands <u>make</u> light work. (<u>hands</u> = <u>they</u> = third-person plural)

> **The present tense shows a habit:**
> Nikki <u>bites</u> her nails.
> He <u>gets</u> angry very quickly. (<u>gets</u> = verb; <u>angry</u> = adjective)
> They <u>laugh</u> at everyone.

> **Use the present tense to discuss a film, book, article, or any literary work:**
> In the movie *Life of Pi,* a boy <u>survives</u> 227 days on a lifeboat with a Bengal tiger, in the Pacific Ocean.
> In the *Harry Potter* series, the dark wizard Lord Voldemort <u>aims</u> to become immortal.
> In the article the author <u>examines</u> the role of the powerful in today's world.

Simple Past Tense

The simple past tense shows that an action or state has been completed before now. Note that the simple past has only one form for all pronouns and nouns, whether they are singular or plural.

Example: <u>help</u>
> I / you / we / they/ he/she / it <u>helped</u> yesterday. (past tense)
> Someone / everyone <u>helped</u> yesterday. (past tense)

Regular verbs change into past tense in the following three ways:

1. When the basic form ends in *e,* add *d* to make the past tense.
   arrive, arrive<u>d</u>;   bake, bake<u>d</u>;   examine, examine<u>d</u>;   live, live<u>d</u>;   close, close<u>d</u>

2. When the basic form ends in a consonant, add *ed* to make the past tense.
   walk, walk<u>ed</u>;   clean, clean<u>ed</u>;   help, help<u>ed</u>;   join, join<u>ed</u>;   wait, wait<u>ed</u>

3. There are a few exceptions to the above rule. For example, when the basic forms end in *b, g, m,* or *p,* add *-bed, -ged, -med,* and *–ped* respectively.

rub, rub<u>bed</u>	grab, grab<u>bed</u>	dub, dub<u>bed</u>	dab, dab<u>bed</u>
hug, hug<u>ged</u>	bag, bag<u>ged</u>	fog, fog<u>ged</u>	clog, clog<u>ged</u>

| trim, trim<u>med</u> | cram, cram<u>med</u> | hum, hum<u>med</u> | slam, slam<u>med</u> |
| clip, clip<u>ped</u> | chop, chop<u>ped</u> | flap, flap<u>ped</u> | sip, sip<u>ped</u> |

> **The simple past tense shows a completed action:**

> I /you/we/they /he/she/it <u>waited</u> yesterday.
> Someone/everyone <u>waited</u> yesterday.

> School <u>reopened</u> yesterday. (<u>school</u> = <u>it</u> = third-person singular)
> Schools <u>reopened</u> yesterday. (<u>schools</u> = <u>it</u> = third-person plural)

Irregular verbs do not follow any rule to form their past tense or past participle

The English language has around two hundred irregular verbs. These verbs cannot be changed into past tense by adding **ed** or **d** to the basic form. The past tense and past participle of each irregular verb can be very different from the basic form. We must learn them, because we cannot apply the regular rule. Please refer to the chart of irregular verbs on page 66-70.

To break is an irregular verb. The past tense of **break** is **broke**, and the past participle is **broken**, not <u>breaked</u> or <u>broked</u>.

> I /you/we/they <u>broke</u> the lamp last week.
> He/she/it <u>broke</u> the lamp last week.
> Someone/everyone <u>broke</u> the lamp last week.

To put is an irregular verb. The past tense and past participle of **put** is **put**, not <u>puted</u>.

> Tim <u>put</u> away his toys yesterday. (basic form = <u>put</u>)
> Tim and Adam <u>put</u> away their toys yesterday. (Tim and Adam = they)

To leave is an irregular verb. The past tense and past participle of **leave** is **left**, not <u>leaved</u>.

> I /you/he/she/we/they <u>left</u> the concert, because it was getting late.
> Someone/everyone <u>left</u> the concert, because it was getting late.

> **The simple past tense shows a repeated and completed action that is not happening now:**

> When we were in college, we <u>visited</u> our friends on weekends.
> He <u>took</u> the medicine regularly till he turned eighteen.

To come is an irregular verb. The past tense of **come** is **came**, and the past participle of **come** is **come**, not <u>comed</u> or <u>camed.</u>

> Many customers <u>came</u> every day to his fruit shop.

> **The simple past tense shows a completed condition:**

> My parents <u>were</u> very proud. (<u>were</u> = linking verb; <u>proud</u> = adjective; <u>very</u> = adverb)
> He <u>was</u> not satisfied with our work. (<u>was</u> = linking verb; <u>satisfied</u> = adjective)

To have is an irregular verb. The past tense and past participle of **have** is **had**, not <u>haved</u>. In the sentence below, <u>had</u> is the main verb and not a helping verb.

> I/you/she/he/we/they <u>had</u> asthma for years.

Common Mistakes in Making the Simple Past Tense

> I was lived here.   **Wrong** (Helping verb <u>was</u> is not needed.)
> I <u>lived</u> here.   **Correct** (Simple past tense)

> They were broke the toys.   **Wrong** (Helping verb <u>were</u> is not needed.)
> They were break the toys.   **Wrong**
> They <u>broke</u> the toys.   **Correct** (Simple past tense)

> She <u>was</u> not satisfy with my work.   **Wrong**
> She <u>was</u> not <u>satisfied</u> with my work. **Correct**
> (<u>Was</u> is a linking verb, because it links the subject <u>she</u> to an adjective, <u>satisfied</u>.)

> They were marry last month.   **Wrong**
> They <u>were married</u> last month.   **Correct**
> They <u>got married</u> last month.   **Correct**
> He <u>married</u> a girl from India.   **Correct**

Simple Future Tense

The simple future tense shows that an action will take place in the future.
This tense has only one type of verb form: **will + basic form**

Examples: will read; will jump; will do; will hit; will play

> I / you/he/she/we/they <u>will play</u> tennis tomorrow. (future tense)
> Someone /everyone <u>will play</u> tennis tomorrow. (future tense)

> **The simple future tense shows a future action:**

> They <u>will go</u> to the zoo tomorrow.
> Her parents <u>will attend</u> the meeting.
> Maya <u>will answer</u> all your questions.
> David <u>will do</u> what he wants to do.

> **The simple future tense shows a future condition:**

> I/you/he/she/it/we/they <u>will get</u> nervous before an audience.
> My friend <u>will be</u> very happy to see me.

> **The simple future tense shows an intention:**

> The committee said they <u>will begin</u> to interview candidates soon.
> The manager said that the job <u>will require</u> me to travel.
> My teacher believes she <u>will need</u> an extra helping hand.

> **The simple future tense shows a possible chance of an action in the future; that is, probability:**

> The blue car <u>will</u> most likely <u>win</u> the race.
> At least five students from our school <u>will</u> probably <u>get</u> a state rank.

Common Mistakes in Making the Simple Future Tense

> She will be satisfy with my work.   **Wrong**
> She <u>will be satisfied</u> with my work.   **Correct**

> The story will be finish soon.   **Wrong**
> The story <u>will be finished</u> soon.   **Correct**

(<u>Will be</u> are linking verbs, because <u>will be</u> links the subject to the adjectives <u>satisfied</u> and <u>finished</u>. Also, the main verb's past participle is used for the passive voice.)

Simple Progressive or Simple Continuous Tenses

The progressive tenses show continuing action. They are made with the <u>-ing</u> form of the verb, called the present participle, and a form of the helping verb <u>be</u>. While the present participle remains the same, the helping verb <u>be</u> changes its tense to show the present, past, and future progressive tenses.

Simple progressive tense = tense of <u>be</u> + <u>main verb</u> in -ing form

Present progressive	Past progressive	Future progressive
I am playing.	I was playing.	I will be playing.
You are driving.	You were driving.	You will be driving.
He is baking.	He was baking.	He will be baking.
She is teaching.	She was teaching.	She will be teaching.
It is jumping.	It was jumping.	It will be jumping.
We are learning.	We were learning.	We will be learning.
They are walking.	They were walking.	They will be walking.

> The present participle or *-ing* form of the regular and irregular verbs is made in the following five ways:

1. If the basic form ends with a consonant, add *-ing* to the main verb.

    ♦ build + ing = building   break + ing = breaking
    ♦ look+ ing = looking   pay + ing = paying

2. If the basic form ends with *one* -*e*, remove the -*e* and add *-ing.*

    ♦ live = liv + ing = living   believe = believ + ing = believing
    ♦ arrive = arriv + ing = arriving   grieve = griev + ing = grieving
    ♦ hope = hop + ing = hoping   prove = prov+ ing = proving

Hoping comes from hope. Hopping comes from hop, which means to jump.

3. If the basic form ends with two *e's,* just add *-ing.* Do not remove the last -*e.*

    ♦ see + ing = seeing   flee + ing = fleeing
    ♦ agree + ing = agreeing   free + ing = freeing

4. Some other verbs require the doubling of the consonant when they end with a *b, g, m, n, p, r, or t.* Add *-bing, -ging, -ming, –ning, -ping, -ring,* and *-ting* respectively.

    ♦ dab + bing = dabbing   cram + ming = cramming   occur + ring = occurring
    ♦ rub + bing = rubbing   run + ning = running   cut + ting = cutting
    ♦ hug + ging = hugging   flap + ping = flapping   sit + ting = sitting
    ♦ bag + ging = bagging   hop + ping = hopping   let + ting = letting

There are many exceptions, such as *soar / soaring, tear / tearing,* and wear / wearing.

NOTE: Do not use progressive tenses to show static states that do not show continuing action or change.

> He is hating his work.   **Wrong**
> He hates his work.   **Right**

> They are needing a computer.   **Wrong**
> They need a computer.   **Right**

> She is knowing all the employees.   **Wrong**
> She knows all the employees.   **Right**

> I am having a house in this city.   **Wrong**
> I <u>have</u> a house in this city.   **Right**

> We <u>are having</u> a child.   **Right**
> (If the speaker is saying that they are going to have a child.)

> We <u>are having</u> a child.   **Wrong**
> (If the speaker is saying that they already have a child.)
> We <u>have</u> a child.   **Right**

The Present Progressive or Present Continuous Tense

The present progressive tense shows action that is continuing now. This tense needs help from the present tense of the helping verb <u>be</u>.

Present progressive tense = present tense of <u>be</u> + <u>ing</u> form of verb (present participle)

- ask =   am asking,   is asking,   are asking
- brush =   am brushing,   is brushing,   are brushing

> **The present progressive tense shows continuing action:**
> I <u>am jumping</u>.
> You/we/they <u>are jumping</u>.
> He/she/it <u>is jumping</u>.
> Someone/everyone <u>is jumping</u>.

> **The present progressive tense shows a continuing condition:**
> I <u>am hoping</u> against hope.
> You/we/they <u>are suffering</u> in this extremely hot weather.
> He/she/ it /someone /everyone <u>is feeling</u> sad.

> **The present progressive tense shows a reality that happens continually, but we cannot necessarily see the action now.**
> Prices of various things <u>are rising</u> everywhere.
> Computer technology <u>is changing</u> at a fast pace.

The Past Progressive or Past Continuous Tense

The past progressive tense shows an action or condition that was continuing in the past and has been completed. This tense needs help from the past tense of the helping verb <u>be</u>.

Past progressive tense = past tense of <u>be</u> + <u>ing</u> form of verb (present participle)

- ask   = was asking   were asking
- brush   = was brushing   were brushing

- **The past progressive tense shows a continuing past action:**
- I / he /she / it <u>was looking</u>.
- You/we/they <u>were looking</u>.
- Someone/everyone <u>was looking</u>.

- **The past progressive tense shows a continuing past condition:**
- It <u>was raining</u> very hard.
- We <u>were freezing</u> in the cold weather that was below zero degrees.
- They <u>were feeling</u> anxious.

- **The past progressive tense shows two past actions happening at the same time:**
- The phone *rang* while I <u>was praying</u>.
- He *hit* another car while he <u>was talking</u> to someone on his cell phone.

The Future Progressive or Future Continuous Tense

The future progressive tense shows a continuing action or ongoing condition that will happen in the future.

Future progressive tense = <u>will be</u> + <u>ing</u> form of verb (present participle)

- ◆ ask   = will be asking
- ◆ brush   = will be brushing

- **The future progressive tense shows a continuing future action:**
- I/you/he/she/it/we/they <u>will be enjoying</u> the island.
- The examiner <u>will be</u> strictly <u>supervising</u> the exams.

- **The future progressive tense shows continuing action at a specific future time:**
- Someone/everyone <u>will be traveling</u> next month.
- In the fifth semester, we <u>will be doing</u> our internships.

	Simple present tense	Simple past tense	Simple future tense	Present progressive (continuous)	Past progressive (continuous)	Future progressive (continuous)
Helping verb	X	X	will	am, is, are	was, were	will be

Examples of Six Verb Tenses

Regular verb look	Infinitive = to look
1. Simple present tense: *(basic form, basic form +* s*)* →	1. I/you/we/they look. He/she/it looks.
2. Simple past tense: *(add -*d *or -*ed*)* →	2. I/you/we/they/she/he/it looked.
3. Simple future tense: *(*will *+ basic form)* →	3. I/you/we/they/she/he/it will look.
4. Present progressive (continuous): *(*am/are/is *+* ing *form)* →	4. I am looking. You/we/they are looking. He/she/it is looking.
5. Past progressive (continuous): *(*was/were *+* ing *form)* →	5. I/he/she/it was looking. You/we/they were looking.
6. Future progressive (continuous): *(*will be *+* ing *form)* →	6. I/ you/we/they/ he/she/it will be looking.

Regular verb <u>arrive</u>		Infinitive = <u>to arrive</u>
1. Simple present tense: *(basic form, basic form + <u>s</u>)*	→	1. I/you/we/they <u>arrive</u>. He/she/it <u>arrives</u>.
2. Simple past tense: *(add -<u>d</u> or -<u>ed</u>)*	→	2. I/you/we/they/she/he/it <u>arrived</u>.
3. Simple future tense: *(<u>will</u> + basic form)*	→	3. I/you/we/they/she/he/it <u>will arrive</u>.

4. Present progressive (continuous):
(<u>am/are/is</u> + <u>ing</u> form)
	→	4. I <u>am arriving</u>.
		   You/we/they <u>are arriving</u>.
		   He/she/it <u>is arriving.</u>

5. Past progressive (continuous): *(<u>was/were</u> + <u>ing</u> form)*	→	5. I/he/she/it <u>was arriving</u>. You/we/they <u>were arriving</u>.
6. Future progressive (continuous): *(<u>will be</u> + <u>ing</u> form)*	→	6. I/ you/we/they/ he/she/it <u>will be arriving</u>.

Irregular verb <u>break</u>		Infinitive = <u>to break</u>
1. Simple present tense: *(basic form, basic form + <u>s</u>)*	→	1. I/you/we/they <u>break</u>. He/she/it <u>breaks</u>.
2. Simple past tense: *(changes)*	→	2. I/you/we/they/she/he/it <u>broke</u>. (~~breaked~~)
3. Simple future tense: *(<u>will</u> + basic form)*	→	3. I/you/we/they/she/he/it <u>will break</u>.

4. Present progressive (continuous):
(<u>am/are/is</u> + <u>ing</u> form)
	→	4. I <u>am breaking</u>.
		   You/we/they <u>are breaking</u>.
		   He/she/it <u>is breaking</u>.

5. Past progressive (continuous): *(<u>was/were</u> + <u>ing</u> form)*	→	5. I/he/she/it <u>was breaking</u>. You/we/they <u>were breaking</u>.
6. Future progressive (continuous): *(<u>will be</u> + <u>ing</u> form)*	→	6. I/ you/we/they/ he/she/it <u>will be breaking</u>.

Irregular verb teach		Infinitive = to teach
1. Simple present tense: *(basic form, basic form + s)*	→	1. I/you/we/they <u>teach</u>. He/she/it <u>teaches</u>.
2. Simple past tense: *(changes)*	→	2. I/you/we/they/she/he/it <u>taught.</u> (~~teached~~)
3. Simple future tense: *(will + basic form)*	→	3. I/you/we/they/she/he/it <u>will teach</u>.
4. Present progressive (continuous): *(present tense of be + ing form)*	→	4. I <u>am teaching</u>. You/we/they <u>are teaching</u>. He/she/it <u>is teaching</u>.
5. Past progressive (continuous): *(past tense of be + ing form)*	→	5. I/he/she/it <u>was teaching</u>. You/we/they <u>were teaching</u>.
6. Future progressive (continuous): *(future tense of be + ing form)*	→	6. I/ you/we/they/ he/she/it <u>will be teaching</u>.

Some More Regular Verbs						
	Base form	Present tense	Present participle	Future tense	Past tense	Past participle
1	arrive	I/you/we/ they arrive he/she/it arrives	arriving	will arrive	arrived	arrived
2	ask	I/you/we/ they ask he/she/it asks	asking	will ask	asked	asked
3	bake	I/you/we/ they bake he/she/it bakes	baking	will bake	baked	baked
4	bark	I/you/we/ they bark he/she/it barks	barking	will bark	barked	barked
5	brush	I/you/we/ they brush he/she/it brushes	brushing	will brush	brushed	brushed
6	call	I/you/we/ they call he/she/it calls	calling	will call	called	called
7	change	I/you/we/ they change he/she/it changes	changing	will change	changed	changed
8	close	I/you/we/ they close he/she/it closes	closing	will close	closed	closed

Some More Regular Verbs					
	Base form	Present tense	Present participle	Future tense	Past tense	Past participle

	Base form	Present tense	Present participle	Future tense	Past tense	Past participle
9	cook	I/you/we/ they cook he/she/it cooks	cooking	will cook	cooked	cooked
10	correct	I/you/we/ they correct he/she/it corrects	correcting	will correct	corrected	corrected
11	cross	I/you/we/ they cross he/she/it crosses	crossing	will cross	crossed	crossed
12	drop	I/you/we/ they drop he/she/it drops	dropping	will drop	dropped	dropped
13	help	I/you/we/ they pick he/she/it picks	helping	will help	helped	helped
14	join	I/you/we/ they join he/she/it joins	joining	will join	joined	joined
15	listen	I/you/we/ they listen he/she/it listens	listening	will listen	listened	listened
16	live	I/you/we/ they live he/she/it lives	living	will live	lived	lived
17	look	I/you/we/ they look he/she/it looks	looking	will look	looked	looked
18	open	I/you/we/ they open he/she/it opens	opening	will open	opened	opened
19	pick	I/you/we/ they pick he/she/it picks	picking	will pick	picked	picked
20	play	I/you/we/ they play he/she/it plays	playing	will play	played	played
21	rain	I/you/we/ they rain he/she/it rains	raining	will rain	rained	rained
22	reply	I/you/we/ they reply he/she/it replies	replying	will reply	replied	replied
23	shout	I/you/we/ they shout he/she/it shouts	shouting	will shout	shouted	shouted
24	stay	I/you/we/ they stay he/she/it stays	staying	will stay	stayed	stayed
25	taste	I/you/we/ they taste he/she/it tastes	tasting	will taste	tasted	tasted
26	wait	I/you/we/ they wait he/she/it waits	waiting	will wait	waited	waited

	Some More Regular Verbs					
	Base form	Present tense	Present participle	Future tense	Past tense	Past participle
27	walk	I/you/we/ they walk he/she/it walks	walking	will walk	walked	walked
28	want	I / you/we/ they want he/she/it wants	wanting	will want	wanted	wanted
29	watch	I/you/we/they watch he/she/it watches	watching	will watch	watched	watched
30	work	I/you/we/ they work he/she/it works	working	will work	worked	worked

	Some More Irregular Verbs					
Basic word	Present tense	Present participle	Future tense	Past tense	Past participle	
1. bear	I/you/we /they bear he/she/it bears	bearing	will bear	bore	borne	
2. become	I/you/we /they become he/she/it becomes	becoming	will become	became	become	
3. begin	I/you/we /they begin he/she/it begins	beginning	will begin	began	begun	
4. bite	I/you/we /they bite he/she/it bites	biting	will bite	bit	bitten	
5. blow	I/you/we /they blow he/she/it blows	blowing	will blow	blew	blown	
6. break	I/you/we /they break he/she/it breaks	breaking	will break	broke	broken	
7. bring	I/you/we /they bring he/she/it brings	bringing	will bring	brought	brought	
8. burst	I/you/we /they burst he/she/it bursts	bursting	will burst	burst	burst	
9. buy	I/you/we /they buy he/she/it buys	buying	will buy	bought	bought	
10. catch	I/you/we /they catch he/she/it catches	catching	will catch	caught	caught	
11. choose	I/you/we /they choose he/she/it chooses	choosing	will choose	chose	chosen	
12. come	I/you/we /they come he/she/it comes	coming	will come	came	come	

Some More Irregular Verbs					
Basic word	Present tense	Present participle	Future tense	Past tense	Past participle
13. cut	I/you/we /they cut he/she/it cuts	cutting	will cut	cut	cut
14. dive	I/you/we /they dive he/she/it dives	diving	will dive	dived/dove	dived
15. do	I/you/we /they do he/she/it does	doing	will do	did	done
16. draw	I/you/we/they draw he/she/it draws	drawing	will draw	drew	drawn
17. drink	I/you/we /they drink he/she/it drinks	drinking	will drink	drank	drunk
18. drive	I/you/we /they drive he/she/it drives	driving	will drive	drove	driven
19. eat	I/you/we /they eat he/she/it eats	eating	will eat	ate	eaten
20. fall	I/you/we /they fall he/she/it falls	falling	will fall	fell	fallen
21. feel	I/you/we /they feel he/she/it feels	feeling	will feel	felt	felt
22. find	I/you/we /they find he/she/it finds	finding	will find	found	found
23. fly	I/you/we /they fly he/she/it flies	flying	will fly	flew	flown
24. forbid	I/you/we /they forbid he/she/it forbids	forbidding	will forbid	forbade	forbidden
25. forget	I/you/we /they forget he/she/it forgets	forgetting	will forget	forgot	forgotten
26. freeze	I/you/we /they freeze he/she/it freezes	freezing	will freeze	froze	frozen
27. get	I/you/we /they get he/she/it gets	getting	will get	got /gotten	got/gotten
28. give	I/you/we /they give he/she/it gives	giving	will give	gave	given
29. go	I/you/we /they go he/she/it goes	going	will go	went	gone
30. Grow	I/you/we/they grow he/she/it grows	growing	will grow	grew	grown

Some More Irregular Verbs					
Basic word	Present tense	Present participle	Future tense	Past tense	Past participle
31. hang (to attach)	I/you/we /they hang he/she/it hangs	hanging	will hang	hung	hung
32. hang (to put to death)	I/you/we /they hang he/she/it hangs	hanging	will hang	hanged	hanged
33. have	I/you/we /they have he/she/it has	having	will have	had	had
34. hide	I/you/we /they hide he/she/it hides	hiding	will hide	hid	hidden
35. hurt	I/you/we /they hurt he/she/it hurts	hurting	will hurt	hurt	hurt
36. keep	I/you/we /they keep he/she/it keeps	keeping	will keep	kept	kept
37. know	I/you/we /they know he/she/it knows	knowing	will know	knew	known
38. lay (to put; to set)	I/you/we /they lay he/she/it lays	laying	will lay	laid	laid
39. leave	I/you/we /they leave he/she/it leaves	leaving	will leave	left	left
40. lend	I/you/we /they lend he/she/it lends	lending	will lend	lent	lent
41. lie (1) (to be; put oneself in a flat position)	I/you/we /they lie he/she/it lies	lying	will lie	lay	lain
42. lie (2) (false statement)	I/you/we /they lie he/she/it lies	lying	will lie	lied	lied
43. lose	I/you/we /they lose he/she/it loses	losing	will lose	lost	lost
44. make	I/you/we /they make he/she/it makes	making	will make	made	made
45. mean	I/you/we/they mean he/she/it means	meaning	will mean	meant	meant
46. meet	I/you/we /they meet he/she/it meets	meeting	will meet	met	met

Some More Irregular Verbs					
Basic word	Present tense	Present participle	Future tense	Past tense	Past participle
47. put	I/you/we /they put he/she/it puts	putting	will put	put	put
48. read	I/you/we /they read he/she/it reads	reading	will read	read	read
49. ride	I/you/we /they ride he/she/it rides	riding	will ride	rode	ridden
50. ring	I/you/we /they ring he/she/it rings	ringing	will ring	rang	rung
51. rise	I/you/we /they rise he/she/it rises	rising	will rise	rose	risen
52. run	I/you/we /they run he/she/it runs	running	will run	ran	run
53. say	I/you/we /they say he/she/it says	saying	will say	said	said
54. see	I/you/we /they see he/she/it sees	seeing	will see	saw	seen
55. seek	I/you/we /they seek he/she/it seeks	seeking	will seek	sought	sought
56. sell	I/you/we /they sell he/she/it sells	selling	will sell	sold	sold
57. set	I/you/we /they set he/she/it sets	setting	will set	set	set
58. shake	I/you/we /they shake he/she/it shakes	shaking	will shake	shook	shaken
59. shine (1) (to be bright)	I/you/we /they shine he/she/it shines	shining	will shine	shone	shone
60. shine (2) (to polish)	I/you/we /they shine he/she/it shines	shining	will shine	shined	shined
61. sell	I/you/we /they sell he/she/it sells	selling	will sell	sold	sold
62. sing	I/you/we /they sing he/she/it sings	singing	will sing	sang	sung
63. sink	I/you/we /they sink he/she/it sinks	sinking	will sink	sank	sunk

Some More Irregular Verbs					
Basic word	Present tense	Present participle	Future tense	Past tense	Past participle
64. sit	I/you/we /they sit he/she/it sits	sitting	will sit	sat	sat
65. sleep	I/you/we /they sleep he/she/it sleeps	sleeping	will sleep	slept	slept
66. speak	I/you/we /they speak he/she/it speaks	speaking	will speak	spoke	spoken
67. spit	I/you/we /they spit he/she/it spits	spitting	will spit	spat	spat
68. stand	I/you/we /they stand he/she/it stands	standing	will stand	stood	stood
69. steal	I/you/we /they steal he/she/it steals	stealing	will steal	stole	stolen
70. swim	I/you/we /they swim he/she/it swims	swimming	will swim	swam	swum
71. take	I/you/we /they take he/she/it takes	taking	will take	took	taken
72. teach	I/you/we /they teach he/she/it teaches	teaching	will teach	taught	taught
73. tear	I/you/we/they tear he/she/it tears	tearing	will tear	tore	torn
74. tell	I/you/we /they tell he/she/it tells	telling	will tell	told	told
75. think	I/you/we /they think he/she/it thinks	thinking	will think	thought	thought
76. throw	I/you/we /they throw he/she/it throws	throwing	will throw	threw	thrown
77. wake	I/you/we /they wake he/she/it wakes	waking	will wake	woke, waked	woken, waked
78. wear	I/you/we /they wear he/she/it wears	wearing	will wear	wore	worn
79. win	I/you/we /they win he/she/it wins	winning	will win	won	won
80. write	I/you/we /they write he/she/it writes	writing	will write	wrote	written

An Example of Twelve Verb Tenses

> We will study the perfect tenses in Part Two of this book series.
> **Example: <u>to help</u> (regular verb)**

1. Simple present tense: → *(basic form, basic form + <u>s</u>)*	1. I/ you/we/they <u>help</u> every day. He/she/it <u>helps</u> every day.
2. Simple past tense: → *(changes)*	2. I/ you/ he/she/it/we/they <u>helped</u> yesterday.
3. Simple future tense: → *(<u>will</u> + basic form)*	3. I / you/ he/she/it/we/they <u>will help</u> tomorrow.
4. Present progressive (continuous): → *(present tense of <u>be</u> + present participle)*	4. I <u>am helping</u> now. You/we/they <u>are helping</u>. He/she/it <u>is helping</u> now.
5. Past progressive (continuous): → *(past tense of <u>be</u> + present participle)*	5. I/he/she/it <u>was helping</u>. You/we/they <u>were helping</u>.
6. Future progressive (continuous): → *(future tense of <u>be</u> + present participle)*	6. I/ you/we/they/ he/she/it <u>will be helping</u>.
7. Present perfect: → *(present tense of <u>have</u> + past participle)*	7. I/ you/we/they <u>have helped</u>. He/she/it <u>has helped</u>.
8. Past perfect: → *(past tense of <u>have</u> + past participle)*	8. I/ you/we/they/ he/she/it <u>had helped</u> yesterday, before we met.
9. Future perfect: → *(<u>will have</u> + past participle)*	9. I / you/we/they/ he/she/it <u>will have helped</u> tomorrow, before you arrive.
10. Present perfect progressive: → *(<u>have/has</u> + <u>been</u> + present participle)*	10. I/you/we/they <u>have been helping</u> for eight years. He/she/it <u>has been helping</u> for eight years.

| 11. Past perfect progressive: (*had been* + present participle) | → | 11. I / you/we/they/ he/she/it <u>had been helping</u> for eight years, until the center closed. |
| 12. Future perfect progressive: (*will have been* + present participle) | → | 12. By next year, I / you/we/they/ he/she/it <u>will have been helping</u> for eight years. |

(For more discussion on verbs, please see *Easy-to-Learn English Grammar and Punctuation, Part 2 of 2.*)

■ ■ ■

Verb Exercises

3A. Complete the sentences with correct tense of the verb <u>be</u>. In some sentences more than one verb tense may be correct.

Example: He <u>had</u> taken the exam last semester.

1. *We_____ at home.*
2. Someone _____ angry yesterday.
3. It _____ barking for a long time.
4. We _____ going next week.
5. The river _____ long and deep.
6. They _____ waiting for their friends.
7. I _____ in the office tomorrow.

3B. Each question has four choices. Underline the correct answer or answers.

Example: (a) <u>I wanted a map.</u> (b) I was wanting a map. (C) I am wanting a map.
(d) <u>I want a map.</u>

1. (a) you are listening (b) you was listened (c) you will listened (d) you listen

2. (a) they are ask (b) I am asking (c) I ask (d) we asks

3. (a) we change (b) they change (c) they changes (d) he is changing

4. (a) it closed (b) it is closing (c) it closes (d) it will closed

5. (a) you corrects (b) she correct (c) he is correcting (d) they was correct

6. (a) we will looked (b) we were looking (c) we was looked (d) we look

7. (a) you tastes (b) she tastes (c) we tasted (d) I am tasting

8. (a) we can played (b) we were played (c) we will play (d) we will be playing

9. (a) they are baking (b) they are baked (c) they were baked (d) they will be baked

10. (a) he is arrive (b) she was arrived (c) he arrives (d) he will be arriving

> **3C.** Complete the following sentences with appropriate tenses of the following words: **shake, go, do, cut, come, break, wear, have, see.**

Example: I did not go to see the movie. My brother <u>went</u> to see the movie.

1. We did not cut the vegetables. She _____ them.
2. We could not see the moon. They _____ it.
3. The child did not break the cup. The maid _____ it.
4. I wore a pink dress, and my sister _____ a blue dress.
5. Everything _____ when the earthquake hit.
6. We did not do the mess. They _____ it.
7. He did not have the money. Someone else _____ it.
8. My brother and I _____ to pay the bill.
9. We _____ our homework when they were playing.
10. Any responsible person will _____ this job.

> **3D.** Complete the letter using verbs and helping verbs.

Dear Sania,

Today I_____ (be) home. I _____ (be) at my desk, and I _____ (write)

this letter to you. How _____ (be) you, and how _____ (be) your family?

These days my office _____ (start) at 11:00 a.m. I _____ (come) home at 7:00 p.m.

We _____ (have) lot of work in the office. Yesterday, I _____ (want)

to go to see the new movie, but I could not. We _____ (go) next Saturday.

Last July, I _____ (have) fun with you when we _____ (go) to eat at

the restaurant. I also _____ (enjoy) when you _____ (come) to visit me at my place. Yesterday, my friend, Tina, _____(ask) me to _____(join)

her at a restaurant for dinner. We _____(eat) at the Taj Mahal restaurant. We also

_____(watch) a movie on TV. Then we _____(listen) to some songs.

After that we _____(go) for a walk. But it started to rain. We _____(be) all

wet by the time we _____(reach) home.

It _____(rain) for four hours. "Why_____(do) you not take your

umbrellas?" _____(ask) my brother.

Now I have to go to _____(pick) up my daughter from school. She_____(stay)

at the day-care center after school. She _____(like) to eat after she_____(come)

home. I _____(make) her some snacks. I _____(hope) to hear from you soon. So

please _____(write) soon.
Love,
Reena

3E. Underline the main verbs. Write *regular* or *irregular*, verb tense, and the basic word. See the example given below.

	Type of Verb	Tense	Basic word
Example: *They hid behind a bush.*	*irregular*	*simple past*	*hide*
1. She corrected the papers.	regular	simple past	correct
2. I drank water after eating.	_____	_____	_____
3. She is helping the children.	_____	_____	_____
4. The house became dirty.	_____	_____	_____
5. The concert began at 8:00 p.m.	_____	_____	_____
6. She dropped the bottle.	_____	_____	_____
7. We are learning computer applications.	_____	_____	_____
8. We saw a snake yesterday.	_____	_____	_____

| 9. He found the keys. | _____ | _____ | _____ |
| 10. They had breakfast. | _____ | _____ | _____ |

3F. Each question has four choices. Underline the correct answer or answers.

Example: (a) <u>it becomes cloudy</u> (b) <u>it became cloudy</u> (c) it was become cloudy (d) it becoming cloudy

1. (a) we drank water (b) we drink water (c) we drinking water (d) we drinked water
2. (a) we have a house (b) we had a house (c) we are have a house (d) we will have a house
3. (a) I found my way (b) I find my way (c) she find her way (d) they finds their way
4. (a) I was told the teacher (b) I will tell the teacher (c) I tell the teacher (d) I telling the teacher
5. (a) You see a ghost? (b) You were see a ghost? (c) You were saw a ghost? (d) You are seeing a ghost?
6. (a) they were here (b) she was here (c) she will be here (d) everyone is here
7. (a) I thinking (b) we was thinking (c) I were thought (d) he thought
8. (a) she read the paper this morning (b) she read paper every day (c) she is reading the paper (d) she was read the paper
9. (a) he was driving (b) he drove (c) he drived (d) he will driving
10. (a) she knowed (b) she knew (c) she was knowing (d) she will knowing

■ ■ ■

4. Adjectives

An adjective is a word that tells us more about a person, place, thing, or idea. An adjective describes a noun, a pronoun, or even other adjectives.

Adjectives answer these questions:
1) What kind? 2) How many? 3) Which one /ones? 4) How much?

We need a **big** box.
> What kind of box? **Big**

There are **five** pastries on the plate.
> How many? **Five**

Keep **these** newspapers on the table.
> Which ones? **These**

I will take **that** purse.
> Which one? **That**

Add a **little** salt, please.
> How much? **A little**

Common, Descriptive, or True Adjectives

A common adjective describes a noun in a general way. Common adjectives add color, mood, and interesting details to the noun.

Some Examples of Common Adjectives

> **angry, beautiful, blue, bright, busy, cloudy, cold, dry, good, happy, hard, hot, long, moist, nice, proud, quiet, red, sad, short, small, strict, wet**

> Tanya is a **tall** girl.
> I had a **long c**onversation with my mother.

- The **strict** teacher scolded the girl for arriving late to class.
- We should not go out on this **cloudy** day.
- Serve these appetizers on a **dry** plate.
- We watched the **beautiful** sunset from the train.

Proper Adjectives

A proper adjective comes from a proper noun, and, just like the proper noun, its first letter is always capitalized.

Some Examples of Proper Adjectives Followed by a Noun

Indian prime minister	**American** president	**Italian** pizza	**Nehru** era
African drums	**English** course	**Hindi** book	**German** cars

- The **Indian** prime minister met with the **American** president.
- We love **Italian** pizza.
- Do you like **Hindi** songs?
- My friend plays the **African** drums.
- I am taking an **English** course.

Position of the Adjective(s) in a Sentence

An adjective can come before or after the noun or pronoun it describes.

- The **proud** and **happy** mother smiled quietly. (before the noun <u>mother</u>)

- The mother, **proud** and **happy,** smiled quietly. (after the noun <u>mother</u>)

- **Proud** and **happy,** she smiled quietly. (before the pronoun <u>she</u>)

- She was **proud** and **happy** and smiled quietly. (after the pronoun <u>she</u>)

An adjective can also come after a linking verb to show a condition or state.

- The bed was **comfortable,** so I slept well.
  (Linking verb = <u>was</u>; it links <u>bed</u> to the adjective, <u>comfortable</u>.)

- He looks **tired.**
  (Linking verb = <u>looks</u>; it links <u>he</u> to the adjective, <u>tired</u>.)

    ▷   She seemed **happy** to meet us.
          (Linking verb = <u>seemed</u>; it links *she* to the adjective, <u>happy</u>.)

    ▷   They appeared **busy** when we met them.
          (Linking verb = <u>appeared</u>; it links <u>they</u> to the adjective, <u>busy</u>.)

    ▷   We were **angry** because he did not show up.
          (Linking verb = <u>were</u>; it links <u>we</u> to the adjective, <u>angry</u>.*)*

Positive, Comparative, and Superlative Forms

Adjectives describe a noun, but how do we know to what extent the quality or amount is present in the person, place, or thing? How do we compare that quality for two or more persons and objects? To make such comparisons, adjectives are used in three degrees: positive, comparative, and superlative. Consider how the following sentences show comparison.

    ▷   Adam is **strong,** but David is **stronger** than Adam, and Tim is the **strongest** boy in school.

    ▷   My English exam was **easy,** but the biology exam was **easier** than the English was, and the chemistry exam was the **easiest.**

    ▷   Maya is **polite,** but Natasha is **more polite** than Maya, and Seema is the **most polite** person in that office.

    ▷   The bus service was **bad,** but the train service was **worse** than the bus service, and the airline service was the **worst** of them all.

The **positive or regular form** stands alone and does not compare nouns.

1. Adam is **strong.**
2. My English exam was **easy.**
3. Maya is **polite.**
4. The bus service was **bad.**

The **comparative adjective** compares two objects or persons. The adjective is usually followed by <u>than.</u>

1. David is **stronger** <u>than Adam</u>.
2. My biology exam was **easier** <u>than the English exam.</u>
3. Natasha is **more polite** <u>than Maya</u>.
4. The train service was **worse** <u>than the bus service</u>.

The **superlative adjective** expresses the highest degree of quality present among three or more things or persons that are being compared. The superlative is never used to compare two objects or persons. The article the comes before the superlative form.

1. Tim is **the strongest** boy in school.
2. My chemistry exam was **the easiest.** (of all the exams I took)
3. Seema is **the most polite** person in that office.
4. The airline service was **the worst** of them all.

Comparative and Superlative Forms with _-er_ and _-est_

1. Generally, if **the adjective has one syllable**, use **-er** to make comparatives and **-est** to make the superlatives.

Positive	Comparative	Superlative
hot	hotter	hottest
brave	braver	bravest
small	smaller	smallest
hard	harder	hardest
nice	nicer	nicest
bright	brighter	brightest
quiet	quieter	quietest

2. If the **adjective is one or two syllables** and ends in **y**, first change the **y** to **i**, then add **-er** or **-est**.

Positive	Comparative	Superlative
easy	easier	easiest
busy	busier	busiest
happy	happier	happiest
pretty	prettier	prettiest
lovely	lovelier	loveliest
friendly	friendlier	friendliest
deadly	deadlier	deadliest

3. For **adjectives with two or more syllables**, use modifiers, words, and phrases before the adjective to show more or less of that quality in the noun.

Positive	Comparative	Superlative
careful	more careful	most careful
polite	more polite	most polite
handsome	more handsome	most handsome
expensive	more expensive	most expensive
dangerous	more dangerous	most dangerous
nervous	more nervous	most nervous
beautiful	more beautiful	most beautiful
interested	more interested	most interested
tired	more tired	most tired
cunning	more cunning	most cunning

4. **Two-pattern adjectives** can be written with a modifier before the adjective or by adding **-er** and **-est.**

Positive	Comparative	Superlative
clever	more clever / cleverer	most clever / cleverest
simple	more simple / simpler	most simple / simplest

5. **Irregular adjectives** do not follow the above patterns. Their comparative and superlative degrees are different words.

Positive	Comparative	Superlative
good	better	best
bad	worse	worst
little	less	least
much	more	most
many	more	most
some	more	most

Comparison between Two Objects or Persons

> My teacher is **nicer** than my brother's teacher.
> Your little sister is walking **faster** than you.
> Her class is quiet, but his is **quieter.**

- ▷ Our situation is **worse** than yours.
- ▷ They reached the school **earlier** than you did.
- ▷ This ice-cream serving seems little, but yesterday he ate **less** than this quantity.
- ▷ It is **better** than going by car.
- ▷ Your approach to work is **more serious** than hers.

Comparison among Three or More Objects or People

- ▷ Yesterday I attended **the best** birthday party ever.
- ▷ Tina is **the nicest** person I know.
- ▷ We are looking for **the cheapest** ticket.
- ▷ We are walking during **the hottest** part of the day.
- ▷ This is **the most crowded** street in the city.
- ▷ She's **the most careful** teacher in the school.
- ▷ This is **the worst vacation** that I have ever taken.
- ▷ Today is **the busiest** day for us.

Nouns as Adjectives

Sometimes nouns and pronouns also play the role of adjectives.

Proper Nouns as Adjectives

- ▷ The **Bollywood** actor acted in over one hundred **Hindi** films.
- ▷ I visited India during the **Nehru** era.
- ▷ My **English** class starts at 10:00 a.m.
- ▷ Let us have **Chinese** noodles for dinner.

Common Nouns as Adjectives

- ▷ The **fruit** shop has many kinds of fruits.
- ▷ She enjoyed the **piano** concert.
- ▷ Some people take an **afternoon** nap.
- ▷ The **vegetable** market is close to our house.
- ▷ The **store** clerk is scanning the credit card.

Pronouns as Adjectives

Demonstrative Pronouns as Demonstrative Adjectives

This, that, these, and **those** function as demonstrative adjectives only if followed by a noun. The pronoun, however, is not followed by a noun.

A demonstrative adjective points out or shows a noun in the sentence. The demonstrative adjective tells us which item(s) the speaker is talking about and how far or close that item is from the speaker.

Demonstrative adjective	Pronoun
▹ Hang **that** <u>painting</u> on the wall, but keep **this** <u>photo</u> on the desk. (<u>that, this</u> = demonstrative adjectives) (<u>painting, photo</u> = nouns)	▹ Hang **that** on the wall, but keep **this** on the desk. (<u>that, this</u> = demonstrative pronouns)
▹ Take **that** <u>toy</u> and leave **this** <u>book.</u> (<u>that, this</u> = demonstrative adjectives) (<u>toy, book</u> = nouns)	▹ Take **that** and leave **this**. (<u>that, this</u> = demonstrative pronouns)

Interrogative Pronouns as Adjectives

<u>**Which**</u> and <u>**what**</u> function as interrogative adjectives and are followed by a noun. They tell us which particular item, person, or topic the speaker is talking about.

- ▹ **Which** <u>movie</u> did you like better? (<u>movie</u> = noun)
- ▹ I do not remember **which** <u>roads</u> are closed today. (<u>roads</u> = noun)
- ▹ **What** <u>ingredients</u> do you need to make the fish curry? (<u>ingredients</u> = noun)
- ▹ **Which** <u>dress</u> will you be wearing for the wedding? (<u>dress</u> = noun)
- ▹ **What** <u>homework</u> did we get this week? (<u>homework</u> = noun)

Possessive (Personal) Pronouns as Adjectives

The possessive pronouns **my, your, his, her, its, our,** and **their** also function as adjectives. They tell us which person, place, thing, or idea the speaker is talking about. The adjectives are boldface, and the nouns following them are underlined.

1. Please return **my** <u>books</u> as soon as possible.
2. I put the keys in **your** <u>purse.</u>
3. She asked for **her** <u>mother's</u> permission before signing up.
4. We are going to **his** <u>office.</u>
5. We are very proud of **our** <u>children.</u>
6. The doll has lost **its** <u>sandals.</u>
7. The ship was on **its** <u>way</u> to England when it sank.
8. **Their** <u>performance</u> was excellent.

❖ **Note the difference between the possessive pronoun _its_ and the contraction _it's_.**

It's = contraction **It's** = **It is** or **it has** = two words **It's** (Apostrophe added in place of <u>i</u> for **it is** and in place of <u>ha</u> for **it has**.)	**Its** = possessive pronoun **Its** = one word. Shows possession. (no apostrophe)
▹ **It's** cloudy today. = **It is** cloudy today.	▹ The doll has lost **its** sandals. Whose sandals? The doll's sandals = **its** sandals **Its** means the doll's = shows possession
▹ **It's** been a busy day. = **It has** been a busy day.	▹ The album had a baby's photo on **its** cover. Whose cover? The album's cover = **its** cover = shows possession

Indefinite Pronouns as Adjectives

Sometimes we have a general idea of what and who we want to talk or write about, but we do not wish to refer to a particular person or object. In such situations we use an indefinite pronoun to refer to persons or things that are not specific or definite.

The indefinite pronouns also function as adjectives. They describe the noun by showing the number of the noun. Some of the common ones are mentioned here: *someone, everybody, much, several, each, many, most, neither, none, both, anyone, either, every, most, they, some, another, few,* and *others.*

In the sentences below, the adjectives are boldface, and the nouns following them are underlined.

▹ **Some** <u>children</u> are sitting under the tree.
▹ **Every** <u>bag</u> goes through the security at the airport.
▹ **Several** <u>dogs</u> came to the picnic area looking for food.
▹ **Most** <u>people</u> stayed at home because of the heat.
▹ We will meet **another** <u>day.</u>

3. Articles as Adjectives

The articles **a, an,** and **the** are considered adjectives, as they give more information about the noun by showing a specific item (noun) in a class or by showing the number of the item(s) in a class.

A and **an** are indefinite articles and point out to any one nonspecific item in a class. (**A** pen from the box. **A** student from my school.)

The is a definite article, and it shows one or more specific items in a class. **The** is used when both the speaker and listener know which object the speaker is talking about. (**The** pen you gave me. T**he** elephant that went by.)

1.   They have **a** <u>dog.</u> They are taking **the** <u>dog</u> for a walk.
2.   My friend gave me **a** <u>book </u>as a birthday present. I am reading **the** <u>book.</u>

In the above example, the article **a** is used to mention the dog/book for the first time, as it means one of the many dogs/books that exists. Then the article **the** is used to refer to that particular dog/book, as the speaker and listener know which dog/book the speaker is talking about.

(For more discussion on adjectives, please see *Easy-to-Learn English Grammar and Punctuation, Part 2 of 2.*)

■ ■ ■

Adjective Exercises

4A: Fill in the blanks with adjectives.
---

1.   A _____elephant just passed this way.
2.   This hotel is _____.
3.   Do you have some _____drinking water?
4.   Mr. Smith is our _____ teacher.
5.   This is a _____bedroom. Do you have anything _____?
6.   I do not remember a lot about the exam, but it was _____.
7.   My phone is _____, and hers is_____.
8.   Sameer washed his car. His car is _____.

4B: Write the opposites of these adjectives.
---

clean_____, tall_____, dull_____, high_____,

easy _____, big_____, young_____, cold _____,

good _____, happy _____, pretty_____,

loud _____, fast _____, expensive _____,

thin _____, selfish _____, wise _____, kind _____,

rough _____.

4C: In the questions below, the words are mixed up. Write the words in the correct order to make sentences. Then underline the adjective(s).

1. card is on / your desk / the / lovely greeting

    _____

2. breeze / the east / blowing /a gentle / from / is

    _____

3. I hope / a good time/ are / having / you

    _____

4. meet / we / week? / next / can

    _____

5. the / English / class? / you / taking / are

    _____

6. sunglasses / are / those / mine / brown

    _____

7. listening / some / to / music / amazing / I am

    _____

8. It / an / book / is / interesting

    _____

9. brother / are / kids / and her / Tina / smart /

    _____

10. I / have /neighbors / good

    _____

11. I / stepped out / noisy party / it is a / so

    _____

12. favorite / show / starts / TV / 9:00 p.m. / my / at

_____

13. 10:00 p.m. / bus / last / the station / leaves / the /at

_____

14. free / the / crowd / attracted / concert / a huge

_____

15. play / cannot / a / day / outside / it / is / we / because / rainy /as

_____

4D: Choose and underline the correct adjective:

1. Are you **interesting / interested** in going to the park?
2. Today's news was **shocking / shocked**.
3. We are **excited / exciting** to take part in the dance.
4. He's the most **wanted / wanting** criminal.
5. I will read you an **amusing / amused** story.
6. You have worked for ten hours; you must be **tired / tiring**.
7. I never saw him study. I am **surprised / surprising** that he passed the exam.
8. I find my job very **satisfying / satisfied**.
9. The roads in this city are very **confusing / confused**.
10. Let us go out and **enjoy / enjoying** the beautiful day.

4E: Put in the correct adjective form.

1. This tea is very _____. (sweetest/sweeter/sweet).

2. Sonia is _____than Tanya. (taller/tallest/tall)

3. Flying by plane is _____ than going by train. (expensive/most expensive/more expensive)

4. Our house is small; I would like to get a _____ house. (big/bigger/biggest)

5. Who is the _____person in class? (young/younger/youngest)

6. She is _____than her math teacher. (more careful/careful/most careful)

7. This bag is the_____ of all the bags. (heaviest/heavy/heavier)

8. Can you be _____ to them than you were yesterday? (nice/nicest/nicer)

9. I want this no _____than Wednesday. (later/latest/late)

10. Our doctor is _____than theirs. (good/best/better)

■ ■ ■

5. Adverbs

An adverb adds interesting details to writing by telling us more about a verb, an adjective, or another adverb.

Adverbs Describe Verbs

An adverb that describes a verb or verb phrase answers the question **when, where,** or **how** about that verb or verb phrase.

1. Where?

The adverb answers the question "**Where?**" about the verb in order to describe the verb.

> Adam is sitting **there**.
> Where is Adam sitting? There.
> The adverb <u>there</u> tells us more about the verb phrase <u>is sitting</u>.

> The milk spilled **everywhere.**
> Where did the milk spill? Everywhere.
> The adverb <u>everywhere</u> tells us more about the verb <u>spilled</u>.

> The fabric measures twelve feet **across.**
> Where does the fabric measure twelve feet? Across.
> The adverb <u>across</u> tells us more about the verb <u>measures</u>.

> Dust is **everywhere.**
> The baby is sleeping **inside.**
> Please take this trash **away.**
> Be careful **near** fire.
> We will meet you **anywhere.**

2. When?

The adverb answers the question "**When?**" about the verb in order to describe the verb.

> Mary will cut the vegetables **tomorrow**.
> When will Mary cut the vegetables? Tomorrow.

The adverb <u>tomorrow</u> tells us more about the verb <u>cut</u>.

▷ The teacher **often** tells us jokes.
When does the teacher tell jokes? Often.
The adverb <u>often</u> tells us more about the verb <u>tells</u>.

▷ They are leaving **soon.**
When are they leaving? Soon.
The adverb <u>soon</u> tells us more about the verb phrase <u>are leaving</u>.

▷ **First,** I will study for English exams.
▷ The storm came **suddenly.** (how and when)
▷ I **often** go to meet my parents.
▷ She takes her vitamins **daily.**
▷ We will **never** visit them.

3. How?
The adverb answers the question "**How?**" about the verb in order to describe the verb.

▷ Tina sang **beautifully**.
How did Tina sing? Beautifully.
The adverb <u>beautifully</u> tells us more about the verb <u>sang</u>.

▷ I replied to her e-mail **immediately.**
How (or when) did I reply to her e-mail? Immediately.
The adverb <u>immediately</u> tells us more about the verb <u>replied</u>.

▷ Please clean this house **nicely.**
How should you clean this house? Nicely.
The adverb <u>nicely</u> tells us more about the verb <u>clean</u>.

▷ We searched the cupboard **completely.**
▷ I **quickly** ran out of the house.
▷ He had turned on the music **loudly.**
▷ She did **badly** on her exams.
▷ They were sitting **quietly.**

Adverbs Describe Adjectives

The adverb answers the question "**How?**" about the adjective in order to describe the adjective.

How?

The answer to **"How?"** is an adverb that describes the adjective.

> My **really** funny friend is visiting us.
> How funny is my friend? Really funny.
> The adverb really describes the adjective funny.

> Sonia is **too** tall to ride the tricycle.
> How tall is Sonia? Too tall.
> The adverb too describes the adjective tall.

> Sameer was **extremely** angry when he heard the news.
> How angry was Sameer? Extremely angry.
> The adverb extremely describes the adjective angry.

> The science questions are **less** difficult than the English questions.
> How difficult are the science questions compared to the English questions?
> Less difficult.
> The adverb **less** describes the adjective *difficult.*

> I have another meeting that's **more** important than this one.
> How important is the other meeting? More important.
> The adverb more describes the adjective important.

Adverbs Describe Other Adverbs

The adverb answers the question "**How much?**" or "**To what degree?**" about another adverb in order to describe that adverb.

How much?

The answer to **"How much?"** is an adverb that describes another adverb.

> Sharon speaks **too softly**.
> Sharon speaks **very softly**.
> Sharon speaks **really softly**.

How softly does Sharon speak? Too softly, very softly, really softly.
The adverbs too, very, and really describe the adverb softly.
In addition, the adverb softly tells us more about the verb speaks.

> ▷ I can break the block **so easily**.
> ▷ I can break the block **somewhat easily**.
> ▷ I can break the block **quite easily**.

How easily do I break the block? So easily, somewhat easily, quite easily.
The adverbs <u>so</u>, <u>somewhat</u>, and <u>quite</u> describe the adverb <u>easily</u>.
However, the adverb <u>easily</u> tells us more about the verb <u>break</u>.

> ▷ She speaks **so slowly**.
> ▷ He works **too quickly**.
> ▷ Our team played **very poorly**.
> ▷ They answered **really honestly**.
> ▷ We walked **somewhat lazily**.

Adverbs at a Glance

The Most Common Adverbs

again, almost, also, always, away, back, even, here, however, just, never, now, often, once, only, over, perhaps, so, still, then, there, thus, too, well, yet

Adverbs That Answer "Where?" about the Verb They Describe

above, anywhere, away, beneath, down, everywhere, far, here, inside, near, outside, there, under, up

Adverbs That Answer "When?" about the Verb They Describe

after, before, daily, finally, first, lately, never, next, now, often, recently, seldom, sometimes, soon, suddenly, then, today, yesterday

Adverbs That Answer "How?" about the Verb or the Adjective They Describe

badly, carefully, cleverly, completely, easily, entirely, fully, happily, honestly, loosely, loudly, quickly, quietly, really, regularly, sadly, sleepily, slowly, tightly

Adverbs That Answer "How Much?" or "To What Degree?" about Another Adverb

amazingly, awfully, completely, extremely, not, quite, rather, really, so, somewhat, too, very

Most Adjectives Change into Adverbs by Adding the *-ly* Suffix

Adjectives:	slow	quiet	clever	easy	loose	tight	loud	bad
Adverbs:	slowly	quietly	cleverly	easily	loosely	tightly	loudly	badly

Adjectives:	sad	happy	honest	sleepy	quick	entire	regular	careful
Adverbs:	sadly	happily	honestly	sleepily	quickly	entirely	regularly	carefully

All adjectives cannot be made into adverbs by adding the -ly suffix.

Adjectives:	big	old	Indian	young	English	fat
Wrong adverbs:	~~bigly~~	~~oldly~~	~~Indianly~~	~~youngly~~	~~Englishly~~	~~fatly~~

Some words function as adjectives and adverbs without adding the -ly suffix.

deep, fast, fine, hard, high, late, long, loud, sharp, short, slow, soon, tight, well

Difference Between Adverbs and Adjectives

How do we know if a word is an adjective or an adverb in a sentence?
An adjective always describes a noun or pronoun.
An adverb describes a verb, adjective, or another adverb.

Note the difference between an adjective and an adverb in the following sentences.

Adjective	Adverb
1. The bus was **early**. What kind of bus? An early one. The adjective <u>early</u> describes the noun <u>bus</u>. <u>was</u> = linking verb 2. I woke up in the **early** morning. When did I wake up? Early. The adjective <u>early</u> describes the noun *morning*.	1. The train arrived **early**. The adverb <u>early</u> describes the verb <u>arrived</u>. 2. The baby went to bed **early**. When did the baby go to bed? Early. The adverb <u>early</u> describes the verb phrase <u>went to bed</u>.
3. The king cobra is a **deadly** snake. What kind of snake is the king cobra? A deadly one. The adjective <u>deadly</u> describes the noun <u>snake</u>.	3. The police were **deadly** serious about looking for the robber. How serious were the police? Deadly serious. The adverb <u>deadly</u> describes the adjective <u>serious</u>.
4. Kim is a **slow** walker. What kind of a walker is Kim? A slow walker. The adjective <u>slow</u> describes the noun <u>walker</u>.	4. Kim walked **slowly.** How did Kim walk? Slowly. <u>Slowly</u> is an adverb, because it tells us more about the verb <u>walked</u>.

5. John is an **honest** worker. What kind of a worker is John? Honest. <u>Honest</u> is an adjective, because it tells us more about the noun <u>worker</u>.	5. John works **honestly.** How does John work? Honestly. <u>Honestly</u> is an adverb, because it tells us more about the verb <u>works</u>.
6. I gave a **quick** answer. What kind of an answer? Quick. <u>Quick</u> is an adjective, because it tells us more about the noun <u>answer</u>.	6. I answered **quickly.** How did I answer? Quickly. **Quickly** is an adverb because it tells us more about the verb *answered*.
7. Natasha is a **fast** runner. What kind of a runner is Natasha? Fast. <u>Fast</u> is an adjective, because it tells us more about the noun <u>runner</u>.	7. Natasha runs **fast**. How does Natasha run? Fast. <u>Fast</u> is an adverb, because it tells us more about the verb <u>run</u>.
8. How is your mother? She is **well**, thank you. <u>Well</u> is an adjective, because it tells us more about the pronoun <u>she</u>. <u>Is</u> is a linking verb. When <u>well</u> describes the health or well-being of a person, it is always an adjective.	8. Your teacher teaches **well**. <u>Well</u> is an adverb, because it tells us more about the verb <u>teaches</u>.

> **Friendly** is always an adjective.

‣ The school principal is a **friendly** lady.
<u>Friendly</u> is an adjective, because it tells us more about the noun <u>lady</u>.

‣ We are on **friendly** terms with the officer.
<u>Friendly</u> is an adjective, because it tells us more about the noun <u>terms</u>.

> **Lovely** is always an adjective.

‣ We received your **lovely** card.
<u>Lovely</u> is an adjective, because it tells us more about the noun <u>card</u>.

‣ A hot chocolate drink would be **lovely.**
<u>Lovely</u> is an adjective, because it tells us more about the noun <u>drink</u>.

> **Good** is mostly used as an adjective.

The adverb form of <u>good</u> is <u>well</u>, but in casual conversation and writing some people use <u>good</u> as an adverb too.

- ▷ **Okay:**   How is your family doing? Pretty **good**, thank you.
- ▷ **Better:**   How is your family doing? Pretty **well**, thank you.

<u>Good</u> and <u>well</u> are adverbs, as they tell us more about the verb phrase <u>is doing</u>.

- ▷ **Okay:**   My work has been going **good** lately.
- ▷ **Better:**   My work has been going **well** lately.

<u>Good</u> and <u>well</u> are adverbs, as they tell us more about the verb phrase <u>has been going</u>.

- ▷   Your teacher is **very good.**
      <u>Good</u> is an adjective, because it tells us more about the noun <u>teacher</u>.

<u>Very</u> is an adverb, because it tells us more about the adjective <u>good</u>.

Positive, Comparative, and Superlative Forms of Adverbs

Like adjectives, adverbs also have positive, comparative, and superlative forms.

Positive degree (describes one object)	Comparative degree (compares two objects)	Superlative degree (compares three or more objects)
fast	faster	fastest
easily	more easily	most easily
brilliantly	more brilliantly	most brilliantly
soon	sooner	soonest
well	better	best
high	higher	highest
loud	louder	loudest
tight	tighter	tightest
badly	worse	worst
far (physical distance)	farther (physical distance)	farthest (physical distance)
far	further	furthest
much	more	most
little	less	least

Sentence examples for adverbs:

- Kim ran **fast**.
- Mary ran **faster** than Kim.
- Natasha ran the **fastest** of the three.

- My brother arrived **soon.**
- My sister arrived **sooner** than my brother.
- My mother arrived the **soonest**.

- John threw the ball **far**. (far over a distance / space)
- Adam threw the ball **farther**.
- Sunny threw the ball the **farthest**.

- Do you have any **further** questions? (Do you have any more questions?)
- His questions were on the **furthest** research of the subject. (His questions were on the most advanced research of the subject.)

- Mini helped us **little**.
- Sonia helped us **less** than Mini.
- Natasha helped us the **least** of all the three.

(For more discussion on adverbs, please see *Easy-to-Learn English Grammar and Punctuation, Part 2 of 2.*)

■ ■ ■

Adverb Exercises

5A. Complete the sentences. Choose from the box. Use each word only once.

suddenly, rapidly, perfectly, easily, carefully, quietly, badly, slowly, nervously, clearly, dangerously.

Example: Sharon opened the door <u>slowly</u>.

1. The bus driver was driving_____.
2. Please wash the glass dishes _____, or they will break.
3. The weather changed _____, and we got wet in the rain.
4. Please sit _____ for the performance.
5. The worker bees move their wings_____ to keep the queen bee warm.

6. Language helps us to share our thoughts_____.
7. I opened my exam report card_____.
8. I hope the directions are_____ clear to all of you.
9. If our team plays _____, we will lose.
10. I can do this job_____.

5B. Underline the adverbs. Write if the adverb describes a verb, an adjective, or an adverb.

Example: It was <u>too</u> dark to go outside. (<u>Too</u> describes the adjective, <u>dark</u>.)

1. I cannot hear anything; you are speaking too softly.
2. Do not talk angrily to any customers.
3. The baby is looking at you happily.
4. Finish your homework quickly.
5. He is a very good musician.
6. She is a somewhat careless teacher.
7. I can never open this lid. It is always tight.
8. She is an extremely clever scientist.
9. Drive slowly on the slippery road.
10. The baby is crying because he's very sleepy.

5C. Complete the sentences by choosing the correct adverb from the box.

---

completing, away, once, somewhat, always, never, almost, completely, one, quite, finally, final, sad, sadly, complete, first, firstly, frequently, often, frequent, well

---

Example: <u>Finally</u> we are going on a vacation.

1. _____ we will read from our English books.
2. My house is far _____ from my school.
3. _____ I forgot my bag on the bus.
4. They _____ told us the horror stories.
5. We understand the situation _____.
6. They visit Canada _____.
7. They _____ canceled the program.
8. The students did _____ on the exams.
9. You must _____ look to your right and left before crossing the road.
10. He agreed to do the work _____ readily.

> **5D.** (1) Complete the following sentences with the correct form of the word below (adjective or adverb); (2) Write if the word in the sentence is an adjective or an adverb; and (3) If there is a linking verb, write the linking verb.

Example 1. good: The food smells <u>good</u>. (Adjective. Linking verb = <u>smells</u>)
Example 2. quiet: The children are doing their work <u>quietly</u>. (adverb)

1. *Fast:* John is a _____ speaker.

2. *Quick:* They got ready very _____.

3. *Beautiful:* The garden looks _____.

4. *Fluent:* Kim speaks English _____.

5. *Neat:* Sonia has a _____ office.

6. *Correct:* The student answered ten questions _____.

7. *Loud:* We could not talk at the party because of the _____ music.

8. *Careless:* That event manager is a _____ organizer.

9. *Easy:* He answered the exam questions _____.

10. *Clear:* The tour guide did not explain it _____.

11. *Regular:* We _____ wrote letters during our college years.

12. *Slow:* They were _____, so we left the place.

13. *Nervous:* He appeared _____ during the interview.

14. *Angry:* The teacher entered the classroom _____, because he was upset.

15. *Good:* Did you eat _____ at lunch?

16. *Bad:* The weather is much _____ now than it was in the morning.

17. *Late:* The package reached them _____.

18. *Little:* She takes much_____ than that for lunch.

19. *Soon:*   We completed the science project _____ and started work on our history project.

20. *Far:*   How _____ do you want to walk?

■ ■ ■

6. Prepositions

A **preposition** is a word used before a noun or pronoun to show location, direction, time, method, or connection.

Examples: **in, on, under, by, above, during, because, from, at, to, about, but, beside, out, up**

We use a preposition in the following ways.

1. To show relation or connection of a noun or pronoun with something or some person
> We saw every corner **of** the shop.
> I am keeping some food **for** her.
> John will talk **to** him.
> I am going to the movie **with** them.
> We all had dinner **except** Mother.
> Go to the bank **without** the dog.

2. To show where a subject is in relation to the object
> My son is **in** school.
> The book is **under** the table.
> The bird is sitting **on** him.

3. To show when an action takes place
> We shall wait **until** Friday.
> We had no electricity **during** the storm.
> **After** school my daughter has a piano class.

4. To show direction
> Sharon is going **to** the store.
> They were walking **around** the neighborhood.
> The children are running **away from** him.
> The train was speeding **toward** us.

5. To show why or how an action takes place
> The post office is closed **because of** the holiday.
> Rosy is taking one month's leave **due to** illness.

> ⟩ He brought his driver's license **instead of** his passport.
> ⟩ The dog is an **addition to** the family.

Types of Prepositions

As shown in the above examples, a preposition can be one word or more than one word.

Examples of one-word prepositions					
about	at	concerning	into	regarding	until
above	before	despite	like	since	up
across	behind	down	near	till	upon
after	below	during	of	through	with
against	be	for	on	to	within
along	beside	from	out	toward	without
among	between	in	outside	under	
around	but	inside	over	unlike	
Examples of prepositions of more than one word: compound prepositions					
according to	away from	except for	in spite of		
along with	because of	in addition to	instead of		
apart from	by means of	in front of	prior to		
as to	due to	in place of	up to		

Prepositional Phrase

A prepositional phrase always begins with a preposition and ends with an object. Most of the time, the object is a noun or pronoun, as you see in the examples below. Note that a prepositional phrase can have just two words: the preposition and the object. Other times a prepositional phrase has the preposition, other words in the middle, and an object at the end.

Prepositional phrases are underlined	Preposition	Object of the preposition
1. The pen is **in the drawer**.	1. in	1. drawer (noun)
2. We are buying a phone **for** him.	2. for	2. him (pronoun)
3. Police cars waited **along** the road.	3. along	3. road (noun)
4. Everybody went **except** me.	4. except	4. me (pronoun)
5. The medicine is **on the table**.	5. on	5. table (noun)
6. He borrowed the suitcase **from** them.	6. from	6. them (pronoun)
7. She was talking **during** the lecture.	7. during	7. lecture (noun)
8. The children cannot attend **without** us.	8. without	8. us (pronoun)
9. I did not enjoy anything **because** of the pain.	9. because	9. pain (noun)
10. Can you go **near** her?	10. near	10. her (pronoun)

Sometimes adjectives, adverbs, and gerunds can be objects of prepositions. In Part 2 we will learn about these. Prepositional phrases give details about the subject and make sentences more interesting.

Prepositional Phrases with Compound Prepositions
The prepositional phrase is underlined.

> ⟩ **According to** the clerk, the office needs a bank statement.

According to = compound preposition   clerk = object noun

> ⟩ We must also give a phone bill **in addition to** the bank statement.

in addition to = compound preposition   bank statement = object noun

> ⟩ They were sitting **in front of** us.

in front of = compound preposition   us = object pronoun

A sentence can have more than one prepositional phrase, as you see in the examples below. Usually the subject and verb is outside the prepositional phrase.

The prepositional phrases are underlined in the sentences below.	Subject and verb are outside the prepositional phrase.
1. A woman with a baby walked into the store.	1. A woman walked.
2. All children except Natasha came to the party.	2. All children came.
3. Reena is walking across the street with an umbrella.	3. Reena is walking.
4. Despite the heavy rain, he came to the office on time.	4. He came.
5. Within fifteen minutes of his call, I transferred the money.	5. I transferred the money.

(For more discussion on prepositions, please see *Easy-to-Learn English Grammar and Punctuation, Part 2 of 2.*)

Preposition Exercises

6A. A sentence may have more than one prepositional phrase and object. Underline the prepositional phrases below. Write the preposition(s) and the object(s).

	Preposition	*Object*
Example: The students got into the bus.	*into*	*bus*
1. They ran between the flower beds.	_____	_____
2. During the holidays we spend time with our friends.	_____	_____

3. Outside the theater you will see food stalls.   _____   _____

4. Past the garage the road turns right to the school.   _____   _____

5. In spite of our exams, we watched the entire movie.   _____   _____

6. All students took part in sports.   _____   _____

7. The English book is next to the clock on the shelf.   _____   _____

8. The woman knocked on the door and went behind the house.   _____   _____

9. Please go up the stairs to the fourth floor.   _____   _____

10. The actor walked onto the stage and gave a speech.   _____   _____

> **6B.** Complete the prepositional phrases.

*Example: **After** the party, we returned **by** bus.*

1. The birds flew _____ the roofs.
2. My friend lives _____ the school.
3. They were hiding _____ the table.
4. The soap is _____ to the sink.
5. The dogs ran _____ the hill.
6. _____ five minutes of my e-mail, she replied _____ me.
7. They ran _____ the river _____ the afternoon.
8. _____ carrying water bottles, we bought them there.

> **6C.** Underline the prepositional phrases in the sentences, and write the part of the sentence outside the prepositional phrase that includes the subject and verb.

Example: <u>At our favorite restaurant</u>, we ate chicken curry and rice.   We ate chicken curry and rice.

1. My teacher gave textbooks to everyone.   _____

2. The bus driver drove away without picking up all the students.   _____

3. You must arrive ten minutes before tests and exams.   _____

4. There are many other stars besides the sun.   _____

5. Our train passed through three tunnels.   _____

■ ■ ■

7. Conjunctions

A conjunction joins words, parts of sentences, clauses, or even sentences together.
In the examples below, the boldface words are conjunctions.

> ▷ Stars are big **and** small.
> ▷ Should we go today **or** tomorrow?
> ▷ The jacket is good **but** expensive.
> ▷ I slept **because** I was tired.
> ▷ Do not go into the rain, **unless** you have an umbrella.

A conjunction connects the following parts of speech:	
1. <u>Nouns</u>	1. Can <u>Mary</u> **or** <u>Adam</u> help with the homework?
2. <u>Pronouns</u>	2. <u>She</u> will go **and** <u>he</u> will stay.
3. <u>Verbs</u>	3. Tina <u>laughed</u> **and** <u>sang</u> during the drive.
4. <u>Adjectives</u>	4. People can be <u>rude</u> **or** <u>kind.</u>
5. <u>Adverbs</u>	5. She worked <u>brilliantly</u> **but** <u>slowly</u>.
6. <u>Conjunctions</u>	6. In the above sentences, *and, all, but, because,* **and** *unless* are conjunctions.
7. <u>Group of words</u> (phrases)	7. The child <u>jumped out of bed</u> **and** <u>came down the stairs</u>.
8. <u>Sentences</u> (independent clauses)	8. <u>They invited us to stay</u>, **but** <u>we cannot go this weekend</u>.

There are four kinds of conjunctions:

1. Coordinating conjunctions
2. Correlative conjunctions
3. Subordinating conjunctions
4. Conjunctive adverbs (or adverbial conjunctions)

Coordinating Conjunctions

Coordinating Conjunctions Join Two Clauses
Coordinating conjunctions connect words, phrases, or sentences of equal importance.

for   and   nor   but   or   yet   so

Many people remember coordinating conjunctions with the letters that make up the word *FANBOYS*.

F = *for*,   **A** = *and*,   **N** = *nor*,   **B** = *but*,   **O** = *or*,   **Y** = *yet*,   **S** = *so*

In the examples below, a comma is used when two independent and complete clauses are joined by a coordinating conjunction. The comma is not used if the coordinating conjunction joins words, phrases, or an incomplete clause.

> **For** can mean *because*.

Although *for* can mean *because*, *for* is a coordinating conjunction that joins two independent clauses in the examples below; therefore, a comma is used before the conjunction *for*.

  ‣ We are happy to walk around. We have been sitting in the plane for nineteen hours. (Two sentences.)
  ‣ We are happy to walk around**, for** we have been sitting in the plane for nineteen hours.

  ‣ Let us not drive home now. It is too late in the night. (two sentences)
  ‣ Let us not drive home now**, for** it is too late in the night.

> **And** joins matching words, phrases, or sentences.

  ‣ Reena is fourteen years old. Adam is sixteen. (two sentences)
  ‣ Reena is fourteen years old**, and** Adam is sixteen.

  ‣ The robber broke into our house. He ran away with lots of things. (two sentences)
  ‣ The robber broke into our house**, and** he ran away with lots of things.
    OR
  ‣ The robber broke into our house **and** ran away with lots of things. (no comma)

A comma is not not needed before the conjunction *and* because the subject, *the robber,* is not repeated after the conjunction, which makes the second clause incomplete and dependent.

Nor connects the second part of a two-part negative expression.

- You will not jump from the diving board. You will not swim in the dirty water. (two sentences)
- You will not jump from the diving board, **nor** will you swim in the dirty water.

- The clerk never checked the document. The clerk never gave any information. (two sentences)
- The clerk never checked the document **nor** gave any information. (no comma)

But and **yet** show difference and join words that do not agree.

- Sunny is a bright boy. Sunny is lazy. (two sentences)
- Sunny is a bright boy, **but** he is lazy.
  OR
- Sunny is bright **but** lazy. (no comma)

- They spent a lot of time with us. They did not want to leave. (Two sentences.)
- They spent a lot of time with us, **yet** they did not want to leave.

Or connects choices or alternative terms.

- Do not phone while driving. Do not text while driving. (two sentences)
- Do not phone **or** text while driving.

- You may borrow the money from a bank. You may borrow the money from a friend. (two sentences)
- You may borrow the money from a bank **or** a friend.

So shows a reason or result that follows the first thought.

- I did not study during the week. I have to study this weekend. (two sentences)
- I did not study during the week, **so** I have to study this weekend.

- I have a cold and cough. I cannot go to school today. (two sentences)
- I have a cold and cough, **so** I cannot go to school today.

Correlative Conjunctions

Correlative Conjunctions Are Used in Pairs

Correlative conjunctions are used in pairs to connect words, phrases, or clauses.

both...and	either...or	neither...nor	not...but	not as...as
not only...but also	just as...so	whether...or	as...as	

In the examples below, two sentences are joined by correlative conjunctions.

> ▷ She was working till 10:00 p.m. Her parents were working till 10:00 p.m. (two sentences)
> ▷ **Both** she **and** her parents were working till 10:00 p.m.

> ▷ The monkey was funny. The clown was funny. (two sentences)
> ▷ **Both** the monkey **and** the clown were funny.

> ▷ You cannot run very fast. I cannot run very fast. (two sentences)
> ▷ **Neither** you **nor** I can run very fast.

> ▷ She does not enjoy shopping. She does not enjoy dancing. (two sentences)
> ▷ She enjoys **neither** shopping **nor** dancing.

> ▷ Sit quietly. If you cannot, leave the class. (Two sentences.)
> ▷ **Either** sit quietly **or** leave the class.

> ▷ You can have fruit juice. The other choice is vegetable soup. (two sentences)
> ▷ You can have **either** fruit juice **or** vegetable soup.

> ▷ My bag was stolen. My wallet was stolen. (two sentences)
> ▷ **Not only** my bag **but also** my wallet was stolen.

> ▷ She exercises in the morning. She exercises in the evening. (two sentences)
> ▷ She exercises **not only** in the morning **but also** in the evening.

> ▷ I am not training for six weeks. I am training for twelve weeks. (two sentences)
> ▷ I am training **not** for six weeks **but** for twelve weeks.

> ▷ That woman is not her mother. That woman is her aunt. (two sentences)
> ▷ That woman is **not** her mother **but** her aunt.

Other examples:

> ▷ **Whether** you like grocery shopping **or** not, you have to get these grocery items.
> ▷ I am going to the show **whether or** not you want to come.
> ▷ The strawberry cake was **as** delicious **as** the pineapple cake.
> ▷ This basketball game is **not as** interesting **as** the last one.

When using correlative conjunctions, follow an equal (parallel) structure after each conjunction.

▷	**Wrong:**	John **not only** <u>understands English</u> **but also** <u>Spanish.</u>
▷	**Right:**	John **not only** <u>understands English</u> **but also** <u>understands Spanish.</u>
▷	**Right and better:**	John understands **not only** <u>English</u> **but also** <u>Spanish.</u>

Subordinating Conjunctions

Subordinating conjunctions join two ideas that are not equal. In other words, a subordinate conjunction joins dependent and independent clauses together to complete the thought.

Examples of subordinate clauses (dependent clauses):

- ▷ **When** I am hungry,…
- ▷ **Until** we leave for the station, …
- ▷ **Before** you go to school, …

In the above examples, the words **when, until,** and **before** are subordinate conjunctions. When a subordinate conjunction is added to a sentence, it makes the thought incomplete. The above subordinate clauses depend on some other words to complete the meaning. Though a subordinate clause has a subject and a verb, it cannot stand alone, and it is incomplete.

Now let us join the independent clauses to the subordinate clauses. The independent clauses are underlined.

- ▷ **When** I'm hungry, <u>I will eat my lunch</u>.
- ▷ **Until** we leave the house, <u>do not pack my computer</u>.
- ▷ **Before** you go to school, <u>you must take your medicine</u>.

Note that an independent clause can stand alone, because it is a complete thought:

- ▷ <u>I will eat my lunch</u>.
- ▷ <u>Do not pack my computer</u>.
- ▷ <u>You must take your medicine</u>.

If someone just said the above sentences, you would not think that any information is missing. By themselves, the independent clauses make sense.

Common subordinating conjunctions

after, as if, although, as, as soon as, before, because, even, even though, how, if, if only, now that, once, for, since, so, so that, than, that, then, though, till, unless, until, when, whenever, where, whereas, wherever, whether, while

As we have seen, *for* can mean *because*; and *for* joins two independent clauses of equal importance, so *for* is described as a coordinating conjunction. The word *because*, however, joins a dependent clause to an independent clause. When *because* is added to a sentence it makes the thought incomplete and that part of the sentence depends on the independent clause to complete the thought. So *because* is a subordinating conjunction.

Sentence examples

Independent clauses first	Subordinate clauses
1. I cannot lift heavy things,	**because** I have fractured my rib.
2. I cannot make fried eggs,	**because** we do not have any eggs.
3. It is my son's birthday today,	**so** I will be leaving the office early.
4. They are playing in the balcony,	**even though** it is very cold.
Subordinate clauses first	**Independent clauses**
1. **Because** of her leg injury,	she cannot climb the steps.
2. **After** I get groceries from the store,	I will rest for two hours.
3. **Since** he fell and bruised himself,	he has been very careful.
4. **Although** her children are doing well,	Mrs. Smith is always worried about them.

(For more discussion on conjunctions, please see *Easy-to-Learn English Grammar and Punctuation, Part 2 of 2.*)

■ ■ ■

Conjunction Exercises

7A. Join the sentences below with the correct coordinating conjunction:
for, and, nor, but, all, yet, *or* **so**

Example: *The people rushed into the store. They had been waiting in the line all night.*
The people rushed into the store, **for** *they had been waiting in the line all night.*

1. The little girl is playing. Her brother is sleeping.

    _____

2. I ran to catch the bus. I still missed it.

    _____

3. We had cleaned the house before they came. The children made it untidy again.

    _____

4. Many dresses were on sale. We did not buy any.

   _____

5. We returned home from the kite-flying contest. We celebrated. We ate snacks.

   _____

6. Is your exam tomorrow? Is your exam the day after tomorrow?

   _____

7. Tina enjoys watching TV serials. Tina enjoys watching movies. Tina dislikes watching sports.

   _____

8. The doctor's office was closed. They went to see another doctor.

   _____

9. They do not have a good income. They bought the expensive jewelry anyway.

   _____

10. I will not sign this proposal. I do not agree with your idea.

   _____

7B. Use appropriate correlative conjunctions in the sentences below.

*Example: **Neither** Sonia **nor** Anthony is taking part in the play.*

1. The form is _____ in my school backpack,_____ in my desk.
2. _____ the adults _____children asked me good questions.
3. You are wasting _____ your money _____ your time.
4. _____you must take your children with you, _____find someone to take care of them.
5. _____my uncle _____ his son works at the hospital.
6. We are paying penalty to change _____ the first flight _____ the next flight.
7. _____you like my article _____ not, you know that it is fair and balanced.
8. _____ you want to nap _____ not, you have to be quiet.
9. She wants to take _____piano _____ violin classes.
10. She will join us on the picnic_____ as a principal _____ as a parent.

> **7C.** Fill in the blanks with a subordinate conjunction and underline the subordinate clause.

Example: <u>While you wash the dishes</u>, I will clean the kitchen counter and the dining table.

1. _____ you start one hour before class, you will be late.
2. Can you tell me _____ she's hiding the birthday presents?
3. _____ we went to the shopping mall, the security guards checked our bags.
4. _____ buying cake at the bakery, we stopped at the pharmacy to pick up my medicine.
5. I don't know _____ we can get forty tickets for the show.
6. _____ he had an umbrella, he never used it _____ it was raining.
7. _____ you get a chance, do come to meet us.
8. The baby started crying _____ soon _____ I put him in the crib.
9. I cannot understand _____ the letter reached so late.
10. Maya listens to music _____ surfing the Internet.

■ ■ ■

8. Interjections

When we feel very happy, sad, angry, shocked, excited, scared, hot, cold, tired, or even plain bored, we may use just one or two words that may not mean much but that carry lot of energy and help us express our feelings. These words are called interjections; they are independent words that come before a sentence. Use an exclamation mark for strong interjections and a comma for mild interjections.

The following interjections express strong feelings.

- **Wow!** What a beautiful monument!
- **Heavens!** He fell. Call the ambulance quickly.
- **Alas!** Those were the days, my friends.

The interjections below show that the speaker wants the person being talked to, to pay attention.

- **Hello. Oh,** I said dinner is served. We are waiting for you.
- **Hey,** watch out or you'll get hurt.

These interjections show a pause or hesitation.

- **Hm…**That is not a bad idea.
- **Aah…**Now I understand it.

Some interjections are just noises or gasps, but they convey the meaning to the listener.

- **Sh.** (Asking others to be quiet.)
- **Whew!** (As if to say, "It's so hot in here!")

Feel free to make up your own. Remember interjections work best when you need to put energy or strong emotions in what you want to say. Otherwise, do not use them. Avoid using them in formal writing.

Some common interjections

aah, alas, darn, dear me, dude, ew, eh, good grief, gosh, halloo, heavens, hello, help, hey, hooray, indeed, my goodness, oh, oh dear, oh my, oh no, uh-oh, oops, ouch, phew, sh, well, whoops, whew, wow, yikes, yippee, yo, yoo-hoo, yuck

■ ■ ■

Interjection Exercises

8A. Place interjections before the sentences below. Many interjections can convey the same meaning. Therefore, one sentence can have more than one correct interjection.

1. _____ I forgot to bring my phone.
2. _____ That is not what I said!
3. _____ What a beautiful sight!
4. _____ Our college team won the competition.
5. _____ You told the supervisor that she is crazy?
6. _____ We cannot meet.
7. _____ My scarf flew away.
8. _____ The roof is leaking.
9. _____ Now, she cannot fool us anymore!
10. _____ Tomorrow is a work day!

8B. Make ten sentences using interjections.

1. _____
2. _____
3. _____
4. _____
5. _____
6. _____
7. _____
8. _____
9. _____
10. _____

■ ■ ■

9. Articles—*A, An,* and *The*

There are only three articles: **a**, **an**, and **the**. They show us that a noun is about to appear. Articles point to the noun or determine a noun; hence, articles are also called determiners or noun markers.

The article **an** is another form of the article **a**. Use **an** in place of **a** before a noun that starts with a *vowel sound*. (More information on this is under the Indefinite Articles: *A* and *An* heading below.)

Sometimes articles are immediately before the noun.

a book	**a** river	**an** elephant	**an** uncle
the student	**the** tea	**the** butter	**the** rain

Sometimes there may be a modifier between the article and the noun.

a great book	**a** long river	**a** big elephant	**a** tall uncle
an understanding uncle	**an** amazing elephant		
the smart student	**the** hot tea	**the** melted butter	**the** heavy rain

Indefinite Articles: *A* and *An*

A and **an** are called indefinite articles because they point to *any one item* in a category of items: for example, a pencil, an elephant, a school, or an orange. Use **a** or **an** to refer to any one person, place, animal, or thing when the reader or listener does not know which definite (specific) noun you are referring to. The articles **a** and **an** are not used before a plural or noncount noun.

For example, use **a** for any one butterfly.

- ⯈ I saw butterfly.   **Wrong**
- ⯈ I saw **a** butterfly.   **Correct**

Butterflies is a plural noun. Do not use **a** before a plural noun.

- ⯈ I saw **a** butterflies.   **Wrong**
- ⯈ I saw butterflies.   **Correct**

Ink-pen is a countable noun that starts with a vowel sound, so use **an** and not **a** for any one ink-pen.

> ⊳ I need ink-pen.   **Wrong**
> ⊳ I need **an** ink-pen.   **Correct**

Ink-pens is a plural noun. Do not use **an** before a plural noun.

> ⊳ I need **an** ink-pens.   **Wrong**
> ⊳ I need ink-pens.   **Correct**

Sugar and *oil* are noncount nouns, so do not use the articles **a** or **an** before such nouns.

> ⊳ He is eating **a** sugar.   **Wrong**
> ⊳ He is eating sugar.   **Correct**

> ⊳ She is buying **an** oil.   **Wrong**
> ⊳ She is buying oil.   **Correct**

Which One to Use: *A* or *An*?

Indefinite article <u>an</u>: The article **an** is used to refer to any one person, place, animal, or thing that starts with a *vowel sound.*

With few exceptions, a vowel sound begins with the letters *A, E, I, O,* and *U.*

an apple   **an** elephant   **an** ink-pen   **an** orange   **an** umbrella

> ⊳ **Wrong:**   She needs umbrella.
> ⊳ **Correct:**   She needs **an** umbrella.
> **An** = any one umbrella out of the many umbrellas that exists

> ⊳ **Wrong:**   I ate orange.
> ⊳ **Correct:**   I ate **an** orange.
> **An** = any one orange out of the many that were available

> ⊳ **Wrong:**   Elephant just passed this way.
> ⊳ **Correct:**   **An** elephant just passed this way.
> **An** = any one of the many elephants that exists

Indefinite article <u>a</u>: The article **a** is used to refer to any one person, place, animal, or thing that starts with a *consonant sound.*

Except for the vowels, *A, E, I, O*, and *U*, all other letters are consonants: *B, C, D, F, G, H, J, K, L, M, N, P, Q, R, S, T, V, W, X, Y*, and *Z*. Generally, a consonant sound begins with a consonant letter; however, there are few exceptions.

a desk   **a** bottle   **a** tree   **a** man   **a** computer   **a** building

> ⊳ **Wrong:**   Give me book.
> ⊳ **Correct:**   Give me **a** book. (<u>a</u> = any one book)
> ⊳ **Wrong:**   I need bottle for water.
> ⊳ **Correct:**   I need **a** bottle for water. (<u>a</u> = any one bottle)
> ⊳ **Wrong:**   We arrived in car.
> ⊳ **Correct:**   We arrived in **a** car. (<u>a</u>= one out of the many car that exists.)

Exceptions to the *A* and *An* Rule

In a few cases, a noun may start with a vowel, but the pronunciation begins with a consonant sound. The following words start with the vowel *u*, but their pronunciation begins with the ***yoo*** sound, which is not a vowel sound. Therefore, the article ***a*** is used before these words.
Examples:

1. **u**nit = (**yoo**-nit)   therefore: **a** unit ✓   an unit X
2. **u**rologist = (**yoo**-rologist)   therefore: **a** urologist ✓   an urologist X
3. **u**nique = (**yoo**-nique)   therefore: **a** unique chance ✓   an unique chance X

Try saying the above words using <u>***an***</u>, and you will realize that <u>***an***</u> sounds awkward.

> ⊳ I have an appointment with **a** urologist.
> ⊳ Walking through the waterfall was **a** unique experience.

In a few cases, a noun may start with a consonant letter, but the pronunciation begins with a vowel sound. The following words start with the consonant **h**, but their pronunciation begins with the **o** sound, which is a vowel. Therefore use **an** in front of such words.

hour = (our)   therefore: **an** hour ✓   a hour X
honor= (onor)   therefore: **an** honor ✓   a honor X
herb = (erb or herb)   therefore: **an** (h)erb ✓   also   a herb ✓

> ⊳ I was waiting for **an** hour at the bus stop.
> ⊳ John is **an** honorable person.

Definite Article—*The*

Use *the* to talk about a _definite (specific)_ person, place, animal, thing, or idea, or when the listener or reader knows the noun you are referring to. You can use *the* for singular and plural nouns and also for nouns that can or cannot be counted.

The is used when the specific identity of the noun is known because of one or more reasons.

a) Use *the* when the noun has been introduced before.

Example 1: The noun *bird* is introduced with the article *a* in the first sentence. In the second sentence, the speaker uses the article *the*, because the reader knows which bird the writer is referring to.

> ⊳   I saw **a** bird fly by.
> ⊳   **The** bird was red in color.

Example 2: The noun *dog* is introduced with the article *a* in the first sentence. Then the article *the* is used, because the noun *dog* has been mentioned before, and the listener knows which dog the speaker is talking about.

> ⊳   My neighbors have **a** dog.
> ⊳   They are taking **the** dog for a walk. Our children sometimes play with **the** dog.

In the two examples below, the article **an** is used, because *umbrella* starts with a vowel. Once *umbrella* is mentioned, the speaker uses the article **the**.

> ⊳   My friend lost **an** umbrella. **The** umbrella has red and blue stripes. If anyone finds **the** umbrella, please return it to us.
> ⊳   I'm eating **an** apple. **The** apple is too big. It will take me a long time to finish **the** apple.

b) If a noun is not mentioned before, but if the situation and the topic of conversation makes the noun's identity clear, use **the.**

> ⊳   After **the** birthday celebration, we put **the** remaining cake in **the** fridge.
> ⊳   I found my watch, but **the** battery is dead.
> ⊳   **The** newspaper boy delivered **the** newspaper at 6:00 a.m.

c) Use **the** if the sentence has more detail about the noun—either before the noun or after the noun—which makes the noun's identity clear.

> ⊳   Our house is **the** last one on **the** street.
> ⊳   Please sing **the** song that you were practicing today.
> ⊳   Where is **the** ticket counter? It is to **the** right.

d) Use **the** when the noun may be the only one of its kind known to everyone.

> ⊳   When **the** runaway train stopped, **the** prisoners escaped.

In the example above, only one runaway train is likely to be in the news at one time, so the runaway train's identity is clear.

e) Use *the* for a unique noun.

Examples: **the** rain, **the** wind, **the** sun, **the** moon, **the** universe, **the** world, **the** Taj Mahal, **the** Great Wall of China, **the** White House

> ⊳   After **the** rain stopped, we started playing again.
> ⊳   **The** earth travels around **the** sun in a path called an orbit.

Since there is only one earth and one sun in our solar system, the article **the** is used before the nouns *earth* and *sun.*

f) Use *the* when superlatives such as *best* or *most* make the noun specific and clear.

> ⊳   Tanya is **the** tallest girl in class.
>   The superlative *tallest* describes only one girl of all the girls in the class.

> ⊳   She bought **the** most expensive jewelry set from the store.
>   The superlative *most* describes only one jewelry set out of the many sets available in the store.

g) Use **the** when talking about *countable but specific* nouns.

> ⊳   **The** water bottles made my purse very heavy.

Also use **the** when talking about *noncountable but specific* nouns.

Examples: **the** future, **the** past, **the** traffic, **the** crowd, **the** oil, **the** salt

> ⊳   Let us not worry about **the** future.
> ⊳   We are late because **the** traffic was moving very slowly.
> ⊳   **The** oil in the frying pan is very hot.
> ⊳   **The** salt in the saltshaker has turned moist.

h) Use **the** for geographical *areas and points* on the globe, except for lakes.

> ⊳   **Mountains:** the Himalayas, the Rockies, the Alps
> ⊳   **Oceans:** the Indian Ocean, the Atlantic Ocean, the Pacific Ocean

> **Seas:** the Dead Sea, the Arabian Sea, the Caspian Sea, the Mediterranean Sea
> **Rivers:** the Nile, the Thames, the Godavari, the Ganga, the Mississippi
> **Deserts:** the Sahara Desert, the Gobi Desert, the Thar Desert
> **Points:** the South Pole, the equator
> **Coasts:** the West coast, the North coast

Do not use **the** for lakes: Lake Superior, Lake Victoria

i) Use **the** if a country or geographical area has a plural meaning.

> **the** United States, **the** West Indies, **the** United Kingdom,
> **the** Middle East, **the** Philippines

Do not use *any article* for country names that are singular:
India, France, Egypt, Spain, Malaysia.

> We live in <u>India</u>, but my parents live in **<u>the</u> <u>United States of America</u>**.
> She is from <u>Canada</u>, and her grandmother is from **<u>the</u> <u>Netherlands</u>**.
> They are going to <u>England</u>, and we are going to **<u>the</u> <u>Middle East</u>**.

j) Use **the** for musical instruments.

> My daughter plays **the** violin.
> My son plays **the** keyboard.
> He plays **the** guitar.

k) Use **the** for classes of people.

> **the** poor, **the** rich, **the** Americans, **the** British, **the** young, **the** Indians, **the** Christians

l) For buildings and institutions, these are the general rules for **the.**

> My children are in school. (*the* is not used)
> I am going to **the** school to watch their performance.
> He is in hospital. (*The* is not used in British usage)
> He is in **the** hospital. (American usage)
> We are going to **the** hospital to see him.

m) Use **the** before ordinal numbers.
(Ordinal numbers show order or ranking: first, second, third…last)

> I was **the** first in line.
> The platform will be empty after **the** last train leaves.

n) Use **the** before decades and centuries.

> ‣   My parents grew up in **the** forties and fifties.
> ‣   Living conditions changed at a fast pace in **the** twentieth century.

When Not to Use *The*

a) Do not use ***the*** before plural or noncount nouns that express "generally" or "all."

> ‣   In many Western restaurants, **the** bread is served before the main dish.

Note that **the** is needed in the sentence below.

> ‣   "I will slice **the** bread," said mother.

b) Do not use **the** for sports.
> ‣   She plays basketball.
> ‣   He plays baseball.
> ‣   We play cricket.

c) Do not use **the** for most illnesses.
> ‣   He has cancer.
> ‣   She has diabetes.
> ‣   I have high blood pressure.

d) Do not use **the** for conditions or illnesses such as *cold* or *headache*. Use ***a.***
> ‣   I have a cold.
> ‣   She has a headache.

e) Do not use **the** for jobs. Use ***a*** because jobs belong to the common noun category.
> ‣   She is a doctor.
> ‣   My father is a writer.
> ‣   He is a teacher.

When Not to Use Articles

a) Do not use **the** or **a** before proper names of people, places, animals, and things except if they are unique.

> ‣   **Continents:** Africa, Asia
> ‣   **Countries** (singular names): Japan, Indonesia
> ‣   **States:** California (in the United States), Punjab (in India)
> ‣   **Cities:** Los Angeles (in the United States), Beirut (in Lebanon), Mumbai (India)
> ‣   **Streets:** Main Street, Park Avenue
> ‣   **Squares:** Taksim Square, Times Square, Parliament Square
> ‣   **Proper names:** Mini, Natasha, Tim, Dell, Toyota, Godrej, Toby

Exception: Use **the** for unique names such as **the** Taj Mahal, **the** White House, **the** Great Wall of China, **the** sun, **the** universe, **the** world, **the** rain, **the** wind

b) Do not use **a** or **an** before noncount nouns. Some noncount nouns like tea, coffee, chocolate, butter, ice cream, and so on are also described as count nouns when they are used with a unit of measure—as one order, one cup, one pound, one liter, one kilogram, one piece, one stick, or one part.

>   **Wrong:**   Mary asked her teacher for **a** guidance.
>   **Correct:**   Mary asked her teacher for guidance.
>
>   **Correct:**   I'll have **an** ice cream.
>   (I'll have one order/one cup/ one wrapped ice cream.)
>   **Correct:**   I'll have **some** ice cream.
>
>   **Correct:**   I'll have **a** tea. (I'll have one order/one cup of tea.)
>   **Correct:**   I'll have **more** tea.

Common noncount nouns

Food and drink	Material and substances	Mass nouns	Abstract nouns
rice, salt, sugar, tea, coffee, flour, water, fish, ice cream, meat, milk, oil, butter, bread, juice	fabric, wool, iron, wood, gold, furniture, jewelry, bedding.	rain, snow, weather, traffic, mud, sand, sky, air, sunlight, nature, wealth	time, knowledge, truth, love, honesty, gravity, energy, wisdom, happiness, freedom, fear, hatred, strength, cowardice, focus, information, pollution

c) Noncount nouns are often used with quantifiers to show the degree or amount. For example, we cannot say, "We need a patience." Instead, we can use quantifiers to express the quantity.

The quantifiers are underlined below.

>   He has <u>little</u> patience. (noun = *patience*)
>   I showed <u>enough</u> patience.
>   You don't see <u>much</u> honesty these days. (noun = *honesty*)
>   The child has <u>plenty of</u> courage. (noun = *courage*)

d) The amount or quantity in some noncount nouns can be expressed using quantifiers or a unit measure. When a unit is used, you can use the article **a** or **an,** because a unit can be counted.

Noncount nouns with quantifiers	Noncount nouns with unit measures. Note the articles a and an.
She drank <u>too much</u> water.	She drank **a** bottle of water.
You must pour <u>enough</u> oil for deep frying.	Please get **a** liter of oil.
We have <u>less</u> time for the project.	We have **an** hour of time for the project.
I want <u>more</u> coffee.	I want **a** cup of coffee.
There is <u>some</u> bread in the fridge.	There is **a** loaf of bread in the fridge.

e) Noncount nouns are never plural. Therefore, do not use any quantifier or words that make them appear plural.

Examples:

- ▹ **Wrong:** There are <u>many</u> pollution<u>s</u> in this city.
- ▹ **Correct:** There is a lot of pollution in this city.

- ▹ **Wrong:** We have <u>four</u> luggage<u>s</u>.
- ▹ **Correct:** We have four pieces of luggage.

- ▹ **Wrong:** She recited <u>many</u> poetr<u>ies</u>.
- ▹ **Correct:** She recited a <u>great deal of</u> poetry.

f) An article is always used before a noun except when another noun marker takes the place of the article. The other noun markers could be possessive nouns, numbers, and some pronouns.

- ▹ She is **a** neighbor.
- ▹ She is **Mary's** neighbor. (*Mary's* = possessive noun)
- ▹ She is **my** neighbor. (*my* = possessive pronoun as an adjective)

- ▹ I'm taking five books to **the** teacher.
- ▹ I'm taking five books to **John's** teacher. (*John's* = possessive noun)
- ▹ I'm taking five books to **our** teacher. (*our* = possessive pronoun as an adjective)

In the examples below, other noun markers have replaced the articles **a** and **the.**

- ▹ We have **a** bag.
- ▹ We have **the** bag.
- ▹ We have **ten** bags.

- We have **several** bags.
- We have **few** bags.
- We have **this** bag.
- We have **those** bags.
- We have **their** bags.
- The warranty is in **its** bag.
- You can check **any** bag.
- You can check **all** bags.
- You may use **either** bag.

■ ■ ■

Articles Exercises

> **9A.** Put the correct article where needed. Some sentences may not need any article.

Example *Question: I just bought new briefcase. Briefcase has number lock.*
*Answer: I just bought **a** new briefcase. **The** briefcase has **a** number lock.*

1. Traffic is quite lot in morning and evening.
2. Homework that I used to get in college took up all my time.
3. Did you go to concert that you and your husband wanted to go?
4. February was coldest month of year.
5. Crowd became restless when their favorite actor did not show up for a long time.
6. Continuous rain made water rise in river.
7. It was interesting movie.
8. Have you seen alligator?
9. Some brave people have visited earth's South Pole.
10. She lives on Park Avenue in New York.
11. Himalayas are nature's wonder, and Taj Mahal is man-made wonder.
12. We saw White House, Great Wall of China, and Lake Superior recently.
13. River Nile empties into Mediterranean Sea.
14. We will be visiting India and United Kingdom.
15. Patient has high blood pressure and diabetes.
16. Why don't you play piano for us?
17. They were playing baseball in rain.

9B. Put a quantifier or an article.

Examples *Question:*   *I have work to finish.*
    Answer: *I have **a lot of** work to finish.*

    Question: *I have piece of silver.*
    Answer: *I have **a** piece of silver.*

1. I gave the beggar money.
2. Sprinkle salt on the popcorn.
3. Please order sugar.
4. The baby will have cake.
5. We have ice cream.
6. Please order kilogram of sugar.
7. We have carton of ice cream.
8. The guest will have slice of cake.
9. We had help on the trip.
10. Do you have salt shaker?
11. Students need guidance.
12. I hope we can get information quickly.

■　■　■

CAPITALIZATION, CONTRACTIONS, AND PUNCTUATION

10. Capitalization

Capitalization means writing in capital or uppercase letters. You have seen that some words begin with a capital letter. But how do we know which words to start with a capital letter? Here are some rules.

1. Capitalize the first word of every sentence.
   <u>M</u>y friends are watching a game on television. <u>T</u>hey are enjoying the game.

2. Capitalize the subject pronoun <u>I</u>.
   <u>I</u> am not watching the game on television, as <u>I</u> have to finish a lot of work.

3. Capitalize proper nouns (proper names). A proper noun is a name *given* to a person, place, thing, or animal. It can be one word or a group of words. Note that the prepositions, conjunctions, and articles (<u>a</u>, <u>an</u>, and <u>the</u>) are not capitalized, but all other words are capitalized.

Anita Johnson	Google	Dell	Taj Mahal
England	Internet	Coca-Cola	Antarctica
New Delhi	Facebook	Toyota	Sahara
Washington, DC	Jupiter	Tata	Himalaya
US Congress	*India Today*	University of Oxford	Great Wall of China

Google, Internet, Facebook, Twitter, World Wide Web, and so on, are proper names given to computer search engines, networks, or websites.
(Capitalization details of sun, moon, earth, and other confusing nouns are explained in Part 2.)

4. Also capitalize common nouns such as *academy, park, river, college,* and so on, when they are part of a proper given name.

Success Time Academy	Yellowstone National Park	Nile River
Fergusson College	Times Square	Atlantic Ocean
Boeing Company	Empire State Building	Lake Ontario
Mahatma Gandhi Memorial	Main Street	Dead Sea
Golden Gate Bridge	Radisson Hotel	Mount Everest

5. Capitalize brand names, as they are proper nouns. Their products—such as cars, jeans, bags, chocolate, or milk—are not proper nouns and should not be capitalized.

   Toyota cars   Levi's jeans   Calvin Klein handbags   Cadbury chocolate

6. Some common nouns are also proper names of persons, animals, places, or things. Capitalize when these common nouns are used as proper names.

   ▷ I met my friend, **Rose,** at the library. (Rose is a proper noun of a woman.)
   ▷ I have a beautiful **rose** in my garden. (Rose is a common noun to show a type of flower.)

   ▷ I am visiting the **Apple** store today. (Apple is a proper noun of an electronics company.)
   ▷ I put an **apple** in your lunch box. (Apple is a common noun to show a type of fruit.)

7. Capitalize all days of the week, all months, all holidays, and festivals.

Sunday	January	Independence Day	Diwali	Ramadan
Monday	February	Chinese New Year	Yom Kippur	Christmas

Do not capitalize names of seasons:

fall (autumn), winter, spring, summer, and **monsoon**
The heavy rains in South Asia from June to October is also called the rainy season or monsoon.

8. Proper adjectives are made from proper nouns, so capitalize proper adjectives.

   Chinese, Japanese, Italian, Arabic, French, Spanish, Indonesian

9. Also capitalize names of nationalities, races, languages, religions, and communities.

1. Nationalities	2. Races	3. Languages	4. Religions	5. Communities
Indian	Hispanic	English	Christianity	Christians
American	Asian	Hindi	Islam	Muslims
Egyptian	African	French	Judaism	Jews
Malaysian	Caucasian	Urdu	Hinduism	Hindus
		Persian	Sikhism	Sikhs
			Buddhism	Buddhists

10. Capitalize titles when they appear before a person's name.

Dr. Tim Smith,	Captain Sameer Roy,	President Barack Obama
Prof. Sara Ahmed,	Mrs. Maya D'Souza,	Prime Minister Manmohan Singh
Uncle Neil,	Grandpa Jeffery,	Cousin Ryan

(For more details on persons' titles and descriptions, please see "Capitalization" in Part 2.)

11. An initial is the first letter of a name used in a person's full name. Always capitalize initials used in names and place a period and a space after them.

Prof. S. M. Ahmed	D. H. Lawrence	Magistrate L. G. Adams

12. Note the difference in greetings of a friendly and formal letter.

Friendly letter greeting	Formal letter greeting
Capitalize the first word and the proper noun.	Capitalize all words in the greeting.
1. Dear Shireen,	1. Dear Mr. Johnson:
2. Dear friends,	2. Dear Students:
3. Dear brothers and sisters,	3. Dear Sir:

13. To close any letter, capitalize only the first word.

Yours sincerely,	Sincerely yours,	Warm regards,	Best wishes,

(Further discussion of capitalization is continued in *Easy-to-Learn English Grammar and Punctuation, Part 2 of 2*.)

■ ■ ■

Capitalization Exercises

---
10 A. Please capitalize as needed.

Example Question: *the pacific ocean is the largest ocean.*
    Answer: *The Pacific Ocean is the largest ocean.*

1. do you know that diwali is a festival in india?
2. like diwali and christmas, ramadan eid is also a festival.
3. i am taking two english classes this summer.

4. we have indians, chinese, french, hispanics, americans, and people of many nationalities in our class.
5. the president of the united states is making a speech.
6. we have ten coca-cola bottles for the party.
7. i asked grandma to check my homework.
8. the english writer h. g. wells wrote some great science-fiction novels.
9. my classes are every sunday in february.
10. i will be flying on american airlines.

■ ■ ■

11. Period, Full Stop, or Full Point (.)

1. Use a period at the end of a simple statement.

    ▷ We planted roses in the garden. (This is a declarative sentence.)
    ▷ You must study for four hours every day. (This is a mild command.)
    ▷ Please walk toward the exit. (This is a request.)
    ▷ Turn right and drive till you reach a stop sign. (This sentence gives instructions.)

2. Place a period and *not* a question mark after an indirect question.

    ▷ **Right:** She wants to know what time is the meeting. (Indirect question)
    ▷ **Wrong:** She wants to know what time is the meeting**?**

3. An **initial** is the first letter of a name. When you use an **initial** in a name, place a period after the initial.

    ▷ John Adams Smith   or   John A. Smith   or   J. A. Smith

4. Do not add a period if the last word of the sentence ends in a period.

    ▷ I will meet you in the coffee shop at 9:00 a.m.

5. An **abbreviation** is a short form of a word. Use a period with most abbreviations that have small letters (lowercase letters).

    Dr.   Mr.   Mrs.   Jan.   p.m.   P.O. Box
    e.g. (example)   Fla. (Florida)   Wash., DC   etc. (et cetera means *and the rest*)

a.m.—*ante meridiem.* These are Latin words meaning before noon. The time from midnight to noon.
p.m.—*post meridiem.* These are Latin words meaning after noon. The time from noon to midnight.

6. Omit the period for abbreviations in capital letters. Note that different names may have the same abbreviation.

- ▷ AD—from Latin *Anno Domini.* Shows number of years since Jesus Christ's birth.
- ▷ BC—before Christ
- ▷ CD-ROM
- ▷ DC—District of Columbia
- ▷ FBI—Federal Bureau of Investigation
- ▷ FL—Florida
- ▷ MA—master of arts degree, or the state of Massachusetts
- ▷ TV—television
- ▷ UK—United Kingdom
- ▷ US—United States (Examples: *US imports*, *US senator. Use US* as an adjective only; otherwise, spell out the proper noun or full name.)
- ▷ USA - United States of America
- ▷ VCR - videocassette recorder

(Further discussion and examples of abbreviations and periods is continued in *Easy-to-Learn English Grammar and Punctuation, Part 2 of 2.*)

■ ■ ■

Period and Capitalization Exercises

> **11 A.** Please insert periods and capital letters where needed.

Example: mt everest is the highest mountain on earth
            Mt. Everest is the highest mountain on earth.

1. is his meeting in jan or feb?
2. dr roy asked you to take one tablet at 8 am and another at 8 pm
3. they were asking when the park will open
4. we took sandwiches, juice, chips, and pastries for the picnic
5. the farewell party is on mon, feb 10
6. julius caesar, the roman leader, reached britain with an army in 55 bc
7. when are you getting your ba degree?
8. most homes have a tv and phone these days.
9. please cross the road at the crossing.
10. please mail this package to mr sk chen
    po box 124
    main st
    ny 20453
    usa

■ ■ ■

12. Comma (,)

1. **Use a comma when a coordinating conjunction joins two independent clauses.**

   ▷ I am eating. My brother is sleeping. (two sentences)
   ▷ I am eating, **and** my brother is sleeping.

   ▷ Tanya likes to read. John likes to watch television. (two sentences)
   ▷ Tanya likes to read, **and** John likes to watch television.

2. **Use a comma to separate three or more words or items in a series. Place a comma before the coordinating conjunction that joins the final item to the series.**

   ▷ Natasha is buying toys, paintings, clothes, jewelry, and shoes today.
   ▷ They read for an hour, played for an hour, and watched television for an hour.
   ▷ We can go to the water park, to the movie, or to the mall.

3. **Use a comma after introductory words in the sentence.**

   ▷ Yes, we are best friends forever.
   ▷ Well, what have you planned for summer?
   ▷ Indeed, it is a great honor to get a national award.
   ▷ No, they have not started selling the tickets.

4. **Use a comma after a person's name when you are talking or writing to the person.**

   ▷ Tanya, your flight is from Dulles International Airport.
   ▷ Maya, did you hear the school bell?
   ▷ You should go to the doctor, Adam, or you will be in pain.

5. **Use a comma after mild interjections. For strong interjections use an exclamation mark.**
   (See page 111 on "Interjections" for more details.)

A mild interjection is separated with a comma.

   ▷ Oh, we need to do something about the damage.

> Indeed, it is a useful suggestion.
> Aah, so that's the trick.
> Well, the case is closed.

A strong interjection stands alone and is used with an exclamation point.

> Oh no! Look at the damage!
> Yikes! I stepped in the puddle.

6. **Use a comma to separate words that interrupt the flow of the sentence.**

> Today, in London, Mini just wanted to rest.
> Parents would, therefore, not want their children to go on an overnight picnic.
> Mount Everest, for example, is the tallest of the eight-thousand-meter peaks.
> The children are sad, however, to see their friends leave.

7. **Use a comma to separate from the main clause an incomplete and dependent phrase (of opposite nature, or contrasting with the main clause).**

> They are busy on weekdays, not weekends.
> Always phone during the day, never at night.
> Aisha, not Sharon, was absent today.

8. **Use a comma to separate a tag question from the sentence.**

> It's an interesting place, isn't it?
> You had fever yesterday, didn't you?
> Tim should attend the class, should he not?
> You have been working all day, haven't you?

9. **Use a comma to write clear sentences and to prevent misreading.**
   (A comma is needed after an introductory dependent clause, and phrases that begin with a conditional *if* are dependent. Also, note that the comma makes the meaning clear.)

> If you can, join the party.
> If you can join the party. (Incomplete sentence.)

10. **Use a comma after a short direct quotation. Note that the comma is placed inside the quotation marks.**

Dialogue tags are expressions such as *he said, she said, they asked,* that are used to quote a person. They are separated from the quote (dialogue) with a comma.

> "I need a vacation," Sharon said.

11. **Use a comma after the dialogue tag and before the quotation marks if the quotation comes later.**

   ▷ Sharon said**,** **"**I need a vacation**."**

   Do not use a comma when the quote is a question or an exclamation.

   ▷ **"**Run to the classroom**!"** Mrs. Williams said**.**
   ▷ **"**When can we play**?"** the students asked**.**

12. **<u>When you omit an important word, use a comma in its place.</u>**

   ▷ I cleaned the tables**;** Aisha cleaned the chairs.
   ▷ I cleaned the tables**;** Aisha**,** the chairs.

   ▷ Sharon is our principal**;** Reena is our assistant principal.
   ▷ Sharon is our principal**;** Reena**,** our assistant principal.

13. **Place a comma between repeated words.**

   ▷ I made the requirements very**,** very clear in the last lecture.
   ▷ Wish you have many**,** many years of happy family life.
   ▷ Whoever can eat**,** eat.

14. **Use a comma between two or more coordinate adjectives that describe the same noun.**
   Coordinate adjectives are equal in importance**,** but each one separately modifies the same noun. Therefore**,** you can use a comma or *and* between coordinate adjectives.

   > If you are not sure about putting a comma between adjectives, change the order of the adjectives or put ***and*** between the adjectives and see if the sentence still makes sense.

Example 1:

1. Drive till you reach a **tall, glassy** building.
2. Drive till you reach a **glassy, tall** building.

3. Drive till you reach a **tall and glassy** building.

▷ **Right** with commas.
▷ **Right** after changing the order of the adjectives.

▷ **Right** even after putting *and* between the adjectives.

Example 2:

1. It was a **confusing, boring, slow** film.
2. It was a **slow, boring, confusing** film.
3. It was a **confusing and boring and slow** film.

▷ **Right** with commas.
▷ **Right** after changing the order of the adjectives.
▷ **Right** even after putting *and* between the adjectives.

15. **Use a comma in dates to avoid confusion.**

   ▷ April 25, 2013 (Set off the day and year with a comma.)
   ▷ 25 April 2013 (Comma is not needed here.)
   ▷ April 2013 (Comma is not needed here.)

Set off of the day from the date with a comma.

   ▷ Our daughter's piano teacher is coming to meet us on Tuesday, 14 May 2013.
     OR
   ▷ Our daughter's piano teacher is coming to meet us on Tuesday, May 14, 2013.

16. **Use a comma after the greeting and closing of a friendly letter.**

   Dear Ali,   Dear Tina,   Dear friends,   Dear family,
   Truly yours,   Love and best wishes,   Warmest regards,

17. **Use a comma between the name of city and state.**
   Fairfax, Virginia
   Mumbai, Maharashtra

18. **Use a comma to separate parts of address in a <u>sentence.</u>**
   Mary Smith, 42 Main Street, Hampton, GA 30228, USA
              ↑   ↑
         No comma   No comma between state and zip code

   For addresses on envelopes, do not use commas after every part.
   However, in some places, commas may be needed to prevent misreading.

Mary Abraham
905 H Wing, Sunrise Towers
42 Linking Road
Bandra, West Mumbai 400026
Maharashtra
India

(See *Easy-to-Learn English Grammar and Punctuation, Part 2 of 2,* for more rules and details on commas.)

■ ■ ■

Comma Exercises

> **12 A.** Please insert commas where needed. Also, use a comma and a conjunction to join two independent clauses.

***Example*:**   He said "It was a good idea to talk to my parents."
    He said, "It was a good idea to talk to my parents."

1. Mrs. Robinson is our English teacher. Mr. Chopra is our music teacher.
2. Maya your science teacher wants to talk with us.
3. Last Saturday for example the guitar player did not show up.
4. No we do not like that ants are crawling around in our house.
5. We are taking a vacation in summer not in winter.
6. I need textbooks for English science geography history and French.
7. Today I want you to deposit the money in the bank pick up the medicines from the pharmacy pick up these groceries and attend your sister's music recital.
8. He shouted "Get out of here!"
9. They are playing very badly aren't they?
10. "It is a great honor to play for my country" he said.
11. If you can sing sing.
12. Danny is a pilot. David is an astronaut.
13. Natasha ate fish for dinner; Katrina chicken.
14. We have a trained honest certified technician to repair your computer.
15. The house inspectors are coming on Monday 17 August 2014.
16. The marathon is on Thursday May 29 2015.
17. Can you find Miami Florida on the map and show me?
18. Her flight in fact is arriving late.
19. Yesterday we had eighteen inches of snow and it was really really cold.
20. My English professor Maryam is a wonderful person.

■ ■ ■

13. Question Mark (?)

1. **Place a question mark at the end of a *direct* question.**

    ▷ What time do you have to leave for work**?**

    ▷ Is this a request or an order**?**

    ▷ When will you submit your homework**?** Tuesday**?** Wednesday**?** Thursday**?**

    ▷ Which movie should we go to**?** Harry Potter**?** Spider-Man**?**

2. ***Do not* use a question mark after an *indirect* question. Use a period.**

    ▷ I want to know what time you have to leave for work.

    ▷ Her mother phoned to ask if she can come to the concert.

3. **Place a question mark after a tag question.**

    ▷ They are interested, aren't they?

    ▷ You will help, won't you?

4. **In casual writing, some people use a question mark to show doubt about information they have. The standard practice is to avoid the question mark and use a qualifier.**

    ▷ Our office building has four (**?**) elevators.   **Non-standard**

    ▷ Our office building has, I think, four elevators.   **Better**

    ▷ My grandmother was born in 1928 (**?**) and graduated in 1950**.** **Non-standard**

    ▷ My grandmother was born perhaps in 1928 and graduated in 1950.   **Better**

■ ■ ■

14. Exclamation Point (!)

Use exclamation points after interjections. Also use them to show emphasis, strong feelings, or a command. Do not use them too much and avoid them in formal writing.

> ▷ Wow! What a grand ship!
> ▷ This curry is too spicy!
> ▷ Sit quietly or leave!

For mild interjections and commands, do not use exclamation points. Use commas or periods.

> ▷ Oh, I I did not get cash from the bank.
> ▷ Just sit down and relax.

(See also page 111 chapter 8 on "Interjections.")

■ ■ ■

Capitalization and Punctuation Exercise

13/14 A. Capitalize and punctuate appropriately.

1. oh no I forgot my homework again

_____

2. did she close the door

_____

3. what a magic trick

_____

4. which dress should i wear blue pink red

_____

5. she wants to know if you will teach the class today

    _____

6. daisy worked on weekends

    _____

7. who is going to help us maria amar rita

    _____

8. he is offering you a job isn't he

    _____

9. stay calm and just correct the mistakes

    _____

10. run the house is full of smoke

    _____

■ ■ ■

15. Apostrophe (') and Contractions

Apostrophe

1. Use an apostrophe to show possession or ownership. The possessive form of singular nouns and indefinite pronouns have an apostrophe and the letter **s.**

Examples of ownership with *singular nouns*:

> ▷ **John's** car is white.
> ▷ The **man's** car is white.
> ▷ **Aisha's** trip to Turkey was good.
> ▷ The **girl's** trip to Turkey was good.

Examples of ownership with *indefinite pronouns*:

> ▷ You can use **anyone's** coupon to get the discount.
> ▷ We found **somebody's** cat.

2. To show plural possession, first make the noun plural and then add the apostrophe and **s.**

> ▷ The **men's** car is white.

If the plural noun ends in **s**, add only the apostrophe after the noun.

> ▷ The **girls'** trip to Turkey was good.

Possession with Singular and Plural Nouns

Singular nouns (one)	Ownership with singular nouns (one person, one thing)
1. one man	1. one **man's** car
2. one girl	2. one **girl's** trip
3. one class	3. one **class's** exam
4. one week	4. one **week's** pay
5. one child	5. one **child's** blanket

Plural nouns (more than one)	Ownership with plural nouns
1. two men	⊳ two **men's** car(s)
2. two girls	⊳ two **girls'** trip(s)
3. two classes	⊳ two **classes'** exams
4. two weeks	⊳ two **weeks'** pay
5. two children	⊳ two **children's** blankets

3. Do not use an apostrophe and **s** to show possession with possessive pronouns: *my, mine, your, yours, his, her, hers, its, our, ours, their,* and *theirs*. The possessive pronoun itself shows ownership. Note that the possessive pronouns below do not have an apostrophe.
    ⊳   **His** car is white.
    ⊳   The white car is **his.**
    ⊳   **Her** trip to Turkey was good.
    ⊳   The plane ticket is **hers.**
    ⊳   Those DVDs are **mine.**

4. For compound nouns or a group of words, add an apostrophe and **s** to the last word.

    ⊳   My **daughter-in-law's** coat is green.
    ⊳   I have **somebody else's** ticket.
    ⊳   Did you read the **Surgeon General's** warning on the cigarette carton?

5. Use an apostrophe to show possession of two nouns.
If two or more people own the same thing, use the apostrophe with the last noun.

Examples: 1) Tim and **Amir's** house (one house)
          2) Neil and **Seema's** mother (one mother)

If two or more people own different things, use the apostrophe with each noun.

Examples: 1) **Rihanna's** and **Meena's** cars (two different cars)
          2) **Anthony's** and **Tina's** computers (two different computers)

6. Use the apostrophe in a possessive noun if the object of the possessive noun is missing but understood.
    ⊳   This is **Mary's** backpack, not **John's.**
    ⊳   This is **Mary's**, not **John's.**

(See also chapter 12 on "Comma" for examples on how to show contrast.)

Do not use the apostrophe for the possessive pronoun.

> That is the **doctor's** stethoscope, not **hers.** (*hers* = possessive pronoun)

7. Use an apostrophe to show omission of letters or numbers.
    > **O'er** the field we go, laughing all the way. (O'er = over)
    > I was born in **'72.** ('72 = 1972)
    > That movie was a hit in the mid **'80s.** ('80s = 1980s)

8. Do not use an apostrophe with verbs. (Possessive pronouns also do not take an apostrophe, as noted in 3 above.)
    > She **teaches** the piano. (*teaches* = third-person singular present tense)
    > My daughter **learns** well. (*learns* = third-person singular present tense)
    > It **snows** often in our state. (*snows* = third-person singular and a factual statement)

Contractions

9. A short form of two words is called a contraction. In a contraction, one or more letters are missing. The apostrophe is used in place of the missing letter(s).
In the examples below, *what's, let's, he'll,* and *we've* are contractions.
    > **What's** the matter? = <u>What is</u> the matter?
    > **Let's** see what happens. = <u>Let us</u> see what happens.
    > **He'll** understand. = <u>He will</u> understand.
    > **We've** explained the method to him. = <u>We have</u> explained the method to him.

1. Contractions using *subject pronouns* **and present tense of the verb** *be*	
I am = **I'm**	he is = **he's**
you are = **you're**	she is = **she's**
we are = **we're**	it is = **it's**
they are = **they're**	

2. Contractions using the present tense of the verb *be* **and** *not*	
I am not = **I'm** not (exception)	he is not = he **isn't**
you are not = you **aren't**	she is not = she **isn't**
we are not = we **aren't**	it is not = it **isn't**
they are not = they **aren't**	

3. Contractions using the past tense of the verb *be* **and** *not*	
you were not = you **weren't**	I was not = I **wasn't**
we were not = we **weren't**	he was not = he **wasn't**
they were not = they **weren't**	she was not = she **wasn't**
	it was not = it **wasn't**

4. Contractions using subject pronouns and present tense of the verb *have*

I have = **I've**

you have = **you've**

we have = **we've**

they have = **they've**

he has = **he's**

she has = **she's**

it has = **it's**

5. Contractions using the present tense of the verb *have* and *not*

I have not = I **haven't**

you have not = you **haven't**

we have not = we **haven't**

they have not = they **haven't**

he has not = he **hasn't**

she has not = she **hasn't**

it has not = it **hasn't**

6. Contractions using the helping verb *will*

I will = **I'll**

you will = **you'll**

we will = **we'll**

they will = **they'll**

he will = **he'll**

she will = **she'll**

it will = **it'll**

7. Contractions using the *subject pronoun and the* **modal verb** *would*

I would = **I'd**

you would = **you'd**

they would = **they'd**

he would = **he'd**

she would = **she'd**

it would = **it'd**

8. Contractions using the *subject pronoun,* **the verb** *do,* **and** *not*

I do not = **I don't**

you do not = you **don't**

we do not = we **don't**

they do not = they **don't**

he does not = he **doesn't**

she does not = she **doesn't**

it does not = it **doesn't**

10. The contractions below are made with modal verbs. They remain the same for all subject pronouns and nouns.

1. cannot = **can't**
2. could not = **couldn't**
3. did not = **didn't**
4. had not = **hadn't**

5. must not = **mustn't**
6. should not = **shouldn't**
7. will not = **won't**
8. would not = **wouldn't**

Examples:

▹ I /you/he/she/it/we/they <u>cannot</u> = I /you/he/she/it/we/they **can't**

▹ I /you/he/she/it/we/they <u>will not</u> = I /you/he/she/it/we/they **won't**

> John <u>did not</u> ask for permission. = John **didn't** ask for permission.
> John and Tanya <u>did not</u> ask us. = John and Tanya **didn't** ask us.

11. **Other contractions**

1. here is = **here's**
2. it is, it has = **it's**
3. it would, it had = **it'd**
4. let us = **let's**
5. there have = **there've**
6. there had, there would = **there'd**

7. there is, there has = **there's**
8. there will = **there'll**
9. what has, what is = **what's**
10. where is = **where's**
11. who is, who has = **who's**
12. who would, who had = **who'd**

(See the difference between the contraction **it's** and the possessive pronoun **its** on page 24 in pronouns.)

12. Note: In nonstandard English, sometimes the contraction *ain't* is used for *am not, is not, are not, hasn't,* and *haven't.*	
<u>**Standard English**</u>	<u>**Nonstandard English or slang (incorrect)**</u>
1. Our college <u>**isn't**</u> what it used to be. 2. <u>**I'm not**</u> doing that work. 3. You **haven't** got any manners.	1. Our college <u>**ain't**</u> what it used to be. 2. I <u>**ain't**</u> doing that work. 3. You <u>**ain't**</u> got no manners. (Using double negatives is not correct English. See also the chapter on "Double Negatives" on page 173.)

(See *Easy-to-Learn English Grammar and Punctuation, Part 2 of 2,* for more rules and details on apostrophes.)

■ ■ ■

Apostrophe and Contractions Exercises

15 A. Use an apostrophe and/or *s only* where needed.

1. Ms. Roy purse is in the staff room.

   Ms. Roy's ...

2. The nurse uniforms are in the changing room. (two answers)

   The nurse 's

3. Everyone gift is on their desk.

   Everyone's

4. It getting dark, so we must hurry.

   It's

5. Im not going to drive in bad weather.

   I'm

6. She cant understand this simple request.

   She can't

7. He hasnt called us yet.

   He hasn't

8. Please write lowercase *is*.

   Please write lowercase.

9. Are these 0s, os, or 9s?

   Are these zeros, os or nines.

10. The printer are not working.

    The printers are not working. / The printer is not working.

11. Its program are boring.

Its programs are boring. Its program is boring (handwritten)

12. These receipt are not mine, but your.

These receipts are not mine, but yours (handwritten)

13. We had lots of fun in the 70's.

14. The windowpane break if you open it forcefully.

breaks (handwritten)

15. Who's interested in joining the writers' club.

who is (handwritten)

Mr. Jones' plea agreement (handwritten)
Mr. Jones's (handwritten)

16. All our doctor are board-certified MD.

---

15 B. Use appropriate contractions for the words in parentheses.

*Example: He (is not) **isn't** going to work tomorrow.*

1. (He would) ___He'd___ love to have ice cream, too.
2. (They will) ___They'll___ let you know.
3. (We are) ___We're___ getting late for school.
4. They (are not) ___aren't___ working in the kitchen.
5. (They are) ___They're___ playing outside.
6. We (do not) ___don't___ want to talk now on this topic.
7. He (does not) ___doesn't___ follow orders.
8. She (was not) ___wasn't___ interested in cleaning her room.
9. It (does not) ___doesn't___ matter what people think.
10. (It has) ___It's___ been a long time since we met.
11. (They have) ___They've___ a good camera.
12. We (have not) ___haven't___ packed for the trip yet.
13. (It would) ___It'd___ be wonderful if you could join us.
14. (What is) ___What's___ the time?
15. (There is) ___There's___ a water fountain behind the tree.

were (handwritten)
we're (handwritten)

■ ■ ■

16. Quotation Marks (" ")

A quotation or quote is a group of words or sentences said or written by another person and used by the speaker to make a point. When we quote someone directly, we use quotation marks around their words.

1. Dialogue tags such as *he asked* and *she said* may come before, after, or even between the quotations. Most of the time, they are separated from the quote with a comma.

    ⊳ My daughter says, "I love you," before she leaves for school.

          ↑   ↑

        Dialogue tag with a comma   Comma inside quotation marks

    ⊳ "Do not blame other children if you get a cold or cough," announced the principal.
    ⊳ "Man is worse than an animal when he is an animal," wrote Rabindranath Tagore.
    ⊳ "Today," my mother said, "we have cereal and omelets for breakfast."

2. Place commas and periods inside the *end quotation marks*.

    ⊳ "Drive carefully and watch out for pedestrians," my mother warned.
    ⊳ "I'm getting groceries," my husband said, "so let me know if you need something."

3. If the quote is an exclamation or a question, use it inside the end quotation marks. Do not use a comma.

    ⊳ "Quick!" my mother shouted to us when she saw the school bus coming.

       ↑

    Exclamation point replaces comma.

    ⊳ Tim shouted, "Come here and see what I found!"
    ⊳ "Did you send your contribution?" he asked us.

                    ↑

             Question mark replaces comma.

4. If the quote is a question, use a question mark inside the end quotation marks.

    ⊳ A news reporter asked, "Did the company shut down?"

5. If the quote is a question, and if you are also asking a question, use only one question mark inside the end quotation marks.

    ⊳ Did the students ask, "Can we have an ice cream party?"

6. If the quote is not a question, but if you are asking the question, then the question mark should be outside the end quotation marks.

   ▷ Are you attending the lecture, **"Tips on Parenting"?**

7. Titles of essays, articles, news, book chapters, stories, songs, poems, radio and television programs (that is, the title of individual episodes and not entire series), and some other creative works need quotation marks. Also, set off the title with commas if the title is not needed to complete the meaning of the sentence. Do not use commas if the title is needed to complete the meaning of the sentence.

In the examples below, the name of the title is not needed to complete the meaning of the sentence, so commas are used.

   ▷ My essay**,** **"Life of an Eskimo,"** is very long.
   ▷ I read an interesting article**,** **"Bouncy Bus Ride? Welcome to Pothole Season,"** in the *KidsPost*.
   ▷ Aunty read us a scary story**,** **"The Train of Horrors,"** last night.

In the examples below, the name of the title is needed to complete the meaning of the sentence, so commas are *not* used around the title.

   ▷ The story **"Eight Signs You Need More Vitamin D"** on *ABC News* had good information.
   ▷ Did you hear the song **"Country Roads, Take Me Home"** by John Denver?
   ▷ Tomorrow, we have a quiz on the chapter **"The Geography of the Nile."**

8. Use quotation marks around special words and phrases.

   ▷ People are getting **"buffet tummies"** from eating at buffets.
   ▷ We had a class on **"morals in life"** throughout our school years.

9. Quotation marks when quoting two people: first use double quotation marks to quote one person, and then put single quotation marks around the second person's quote.

   ▷ Abraham said**,** **"Sara phoned and screamed,** **'It's an emergency!'"**

                 ↑   ↑

   Abraham's quote in double quotation   Sara's quote in single quotation marks inside the double quotation

10. Do not use quotation marks when you quote someone indirectly or when you do not use their exact words.

    ▷ The principal told the students not to blame others if they got a cold or cough.
    ▷ He asked us if we had sent our contribution.

(See *Easy-to-Learn English Grammar and Punctuation, Part 2 of 2,* for more rules and details on quotation marks.)

■ ■ ■

Quotation Marks Exercise

16 A. Use quotation marks, other punctuation, and capitalization where needed.

1. turn the volume of the tv down shouted my sister from her room.

_____

2. he asked me to explain my article to him.

_____

3. now the lawyer said we have to think about this case in a different way

_____

4. hurry before the sale ends our store is advertising

_____

5. the manager asked how many customers visited our store today

_____

6. did your teacher ask why are you riding the bus today

_____

7. are you attending the cookery class making birthday cakes

_____

8. your essay a history of cars has many grammar mistakes

_____

9. the story spot workers who steal in life today magazine is interesting

_____

10. the boss said tina wrote I am resigning immediately

_____

■ ■ ■

17. Semicolon (;)

1. The semicolon functions as a period. When two sentences (or complete and independent clauses) are equal or close in meaning, use a semicolon to join them.

In the examples below, the semicolon joins related sentences.

   ▷ I am leaving for office; I have a lot of work to finish today.
   ▷ The air-conditioner is not working; we can sit outdoors, as it is more pleasant outside.
   ▷ They are stuck in traffic; they just called to say they will be here in fifteen minutes.

2. The above sentences can also be joined by a conjunctive adverb. Use a semicolon before and a comma after the conjunctive adverb.

   ▷ I am leaving for office; moreover, I have a lot of work to finish today.
   ▷ The air-conditioner is not working; anyway, we can sit outdoors as it is more pleasant outside.
   ▷ They were stuck in traffic; however, they just called to say they will be here in ten minutes.

3. Similarly, use a semicolon before and a comma after an introductory word (or words) when they are followed by a complete sentence or a list. Examples of introductory words: *however, therefore, for example, for instance, that is, namely.*

   ▷ You have to bring important items to class; for example, pens, pencils, notebooks, textbooks, and a geometry box are always needed.
   ▷ Some of my class students did very well in the spelling contest; namely, Saniya, Tina, David, and Adam won the first four prizes.

4. Use semicolons to separate individual items in a series of items that has commas.

   ▷ The guest speakers are Seema Abraham, principal at Reese School; Neal Robinson, director at Parkview Hospital; and Maya D'Souza, manager at Diamond Properties.

5. Generally a comma is placed before a coordinating conjunction when it separates two independent clauses. However, sometimes, to separate the sentences clearly, a semicolon and a coordinating conjunction is used, especially if one or both sentences have a comma.

> If you like this coat, I will buy it for you; and you will have to wear it every day in winter.
> The wedding preparations were complete; but some important people arrived late, including the bridegroom, so the ceremony was delayed.

■ ■ ■

Semicolon Exercise

17A. Use a semicolon and comma where needed.

1. This month I will read your essays next month I will grade them.
2. If she likes the teacher she will continue the class and if I have the time I will take her to class.
3. The airport security took too much time therefore I missed my flight.
4. They are painting my office nevertheless I still have to work from the office.
5. I'm flying to India he's flying to Japan.
6. To travel abroad you need three important things for example a passport visa and ticket are definitely needed.
7. When I visit the doctor he answers my questions but he does not return my phone calls.
8. For this function we are inviting Daisy the actress Adam a popular model Tanya a TV host and Sunny the famous singer.
9. I saw two stray cats today I usually notice only stray dogs every day.
10. I need these things namely an Internet connection a cell phone service cable TV and taxi service.

■ ■ ■

18. Colon (:)

The colon is an introduction mark that points to the rest of the sentence.
Always use a colon only after a complete sentence. After the colon, you may start the list, items, series, or sentence with a capital or a lower-case letter, but use the same style throughout the text.

1. Use a colon at the end of a complete sentence to introduce lists or series.
   - To make the cake we need these ingredients: flour, butter, sugar, eggs, and vanilla essence.
   - Before you get married, you must be able to do the following: have a decent job, afford a living place, and be a responsible person.

2. Use a colon to add detail.
   - The nurse did the child's physical exam: she weighed the child, checked his temperature and blood pressure, examined his throat, and asked if he was coughing or hurting.

3. Use a colon to introduce a quotation. The quotation always begins with a capital letter, even if the first letter was not capitalized by the author you're quoting.
   - The teacher asked us to consider Emerson's quote: "Use what language you will, you can never say anything but what you are."
   - I believe in this quote by a Greek playwright: "Ugly deeds are taught by ugly deeds."

4. For long quotations do not use quotation marks. Indent the text from both sides and write the quote after the colon.
   - At the meeting, the manager made this announcement:
   I'm very happy with the performance of my team, so each of you will get a good bonus this year. We will also celebrate with a good party in December and you are most welcome to bring your family members. I'm glad that many of you have been promoted and others will soon get their promotions. I hope to see the same or even better performance in the coming year. Thank you.

5. Use a colon after a salutation in a business letter.
   Dear Madam: Dear Mr. Johnson: Dear President:

6. Use a colon between a title and subtitle.
   Eating Giants: Elephants
   Space: Explore the Stars

7. Use a colon between the hour and minutes when you write time.
    8:30 a.m.   6:43 p.m.

8. Use a colon to show ratio and proportions.
    ▷ To make the cake, the proportion of flour to sugar is 2:1.
    ▷ The ratio of men to women in our workplace is 3:4.

9. Do not use a colon with incomplete sentences. Also do not use a colon after verbs, prepositions, and words such as *such as, including, for example*, and *for instance.*
    ▷ **Wrong:**   My shopping list consists of: shampoo, toothpaste, shaving cream, blades, and a comb.
    ▷ **Right:**   My shopping list consists of shampoo, toothpaste, shaving cream, blades, and a comb.
    ▷ **Wrong:**   We should invite many people including: musicians, singers, writers, film directors, and actors.
    ▷ **Right:**   We should invite many people, including musicians, singers, writers, film directors, and actors.

(See *Easy-to-Learn English Grammar and Punctuation, Part 2 of 2*, for more rules and details on colons.)

■ ■ ■

Colon Exercise

18A. Insert correct punctuation, including the colon, where needed.

Example:
Question: Next month we have tests in these subjects geography history physics chemistry English and biology
Answer: Next month, we have tests in these subjects: geography, history, physics, chemistry, English, and biology.

1. The actors in the play are Mary the mother Anthony the father Daisy the daughter Shirin Marys friend and Sunny Shirin's husband
2. The day-care center needs items such as bottles diapers tissue boxes and snacks
3. Dear Sir
4. She made it very clear to all of us I'm not attending the meeting
5. Kim traveled to Japan Malaysia Singapore and India
6. I am reading the book *Family How to Keep the Love*
7. The project leader started the meeting with this quote in order to succeed you have to believe that you can.
8. He has to be at the office at 830 am

9. Before we left for the trip we checked for the following passport ticket drivers license medicines laptop computer phone and chargers

10. The ratio of unemployed people to employed stands at 4 to 1.

■ ■ ■

19. Hyphen (-)

Hyphen and Compound Noun

When two or more words work as one unit to express one idea, it is called a **compound.**
A hyphen is a short line that joins *two or more words* to make a compound.
Examples: *great-grandmother, mid-July, ex-minister, all-rounder, self-control*

Compound nouns can be two words, one word, or a hyphenated word. If the compound word is not in the dictionary, write it as two words.

One-word compound nouns (closed compound)	Two words (open compound)	Hyphenated compound nouns
fruitcake	ice cream	court-martial
handbag	post office	father-in-law
newspaper	seat belt	great-grandmother
dishwasher	soda pop	wire-cutter
screenplay	train station	self-conscious
skyscraper	high school	well-wisher

Use a hyphen in a compound noun when the noun is used as an adjective.

> These **ice-cream** cones are very small.
> The compound noun *ice cream* has two words; however, in the above sentence, *ice-cream* has a hyphen, because it is used as an adjective to describe the noun *cones.*

> What is the **post-office** address?
> The compound noun *post office* has two words; however, in the above sentence, *post-office* has a hyphen, because it is used as an adjective to describe the noun *address.*

> **Dining-room** tables come in many shapes.
> The compound noun *dining room* has two words; however, in the above sentence, *dining-room* has a hyphen, because it is used as an adjective to describe the noun *tables.*

Hyphen and Compound Adjective

Use a hyphen to join adjectives when they come before a noun *as one unit* and modify that noun. When the compound adjective comes after the noun, the hyphen may or may not be used, depending on the adjective or sentence.

> ⊳ The **good-looking** actor gave me his autograph. (*actor* = noun)
> ⊳ The girl sitting by the window is **good-looking**.
>   (According to the dictionary, the compound adjective *good-looking* is always hyphenated.)

> ⊳ The auditorium was packed with **seventeen-year-old** students. (*students* = noun)
> ⊳ I gave the tickets to students who were **seventeen years old**.
>   (no hyphen)

> ⊳ We have many **English-speaking** people in this group. (*people* = noun)
> ⊳ Many people in this group are **English-speaking**.
>   (A hyphen is needed to avoid confusion)

> ⊳ This is an **air-conditioned** hotel.
> ⊳ The hotel is **air-conditioned.**

Some words end in **-ly,** but they are not adverbs; they are adjectives.
Examples: *friendly, deadly, lovely,* and *early* (depending on how *early* is used.)
Use a hyphen when such words are part of the compound adjective *that expresses one idea and modify one noun.*

> ⊳ I met a **lovely-looking** lady.

The compound adjective *lovely-looking* is one idea, and it modifies the noun *lady.*
(If the compound word has an adverb ending in **-ly**, do not use a hyphen, even if it comes before the noun.
See the heading below: Hyphen and Compound Modifier with an Adverb.)

Hyphen and Compound Verb

Compound verbs are hyphenated or one word. If the basic form of the verb has a hyphen, use a hyphen for other forms of the verb. (Phrasal verbs are different from compound verbs. See *Part 2* of this book if you are interested in learning about phrasal verbs.)

> ⊳ To **cross-examine** this witness is a challenge.
> ⊳ This witness is a challenge to **cross-examine.**

> ⊳ We **dry-cleaned** these curtains last week.
> ⊳ These curtains were **dry-cleaned** last week.

> ⊳ How do they plan to **bulldoze** this forest?
> ⊳ The forest was **bulldozed** years ago.

Hyphen and Compound Modifier with an Adverb

If the compound word <u>has an adverb ending in -**ly**</u>, do not use a hyphen, even if it comes before the noun.

> ▷ Give a bonus to the **honestly working** clerk.
> The phrase *honestly working* is not one idea, because the adverb *honestly* modifies *working*, and *working* modifies the noun *clerk*. Therefore, a hyphen is not used.

> ▷ In this country, we have a **strictly enforced** law.
> The phrase *strictly enforced* is not one unit. The adverb *strictly* modifies *enforced*, and *enforced* modifies *law*, so a hyphen is not used.

If the compound word has an adverb that *does not end in* **-ly**, use a hyphen if it comes before the noun. Do not hyphenate if it comes after the noun.

> ▷ In this country, we have a **well-enforced** law.
> ▷ In this country, the law is **well enforced.**

> ▷ Many **well-known** scientists attended the conference.
> *But*
> ▷ The bad effects of alcohol are **well known.**

The modifier *well-enforced* is one idea, and it modifies the noun *law*.
The modifier *well-known* is one idea, and it modifies the noun *scientists*, so a hyphen is used when the modifier comes before the noun.

Hyphen and Numbers

Hyphenate numbers from twenty-one through ninety-nine, even if they are part of a bigger number. Other numbers are open.

sixty-five	**twenty-first**	**three hundred sixty-seven**	**thirty-six** million
six hundred	seven thousand	two hundred thousand	one hundred and ten

Use a hyphen to spell out decades.

nineteen-fifties
eighteen-nineties

Hyphenate if a number is part of a compound adjective that modifies a noun.

Fifth-floor apartment (Names of apartments, streets, avenues, and so forth, are capitalized.)
fifty-piece orchestra

twenty-mile distance
third-to-last row
second-best performance (The performance was **second best.**)

Use a hyphen to show fractions in words.

one-fourth cup, **three-fourths** tablespoon, one **twenty-fifth** part, a **half-hour** class

Hyphen and Prefixes

A prefix is a letter or group of letters added to the beginning of a word to change its meaning.

Use a hyphen with these prefixes only: **self-**, **all-**, **ex-**, **half-**, **quarter-**, **quasi-**, and the suffix
-elect. However, some words are close compounds, so check your dictionary.

all-clear	**ex-minister**	**half-term** but **halfhearted**
quasi-official	**self-conscious**	**president-elect** (only suffix with a hyphen)

The words *selfish, selfless, selfhood* do not have a hyphen, because *self* is not a prefix in these words.

Do not hyphenate positions and ranks in military and government.
vice president   **prime minister**   **major general**

Use a hyphen between a prefix and a proper noun or adjective.
mid-August   **non-Egyptian**   **pan-African**   **pro-American**

Use a hyphen between a capital letter and a word.
        X-ray   **T-shirt**

Use a hyphen to make your writing clear.
> The word ***recreation*** means to relax or enjoy.
> The word ***re-creation*** means to create again.

Recreation and *re-creation* have different pronunciations as well.

> The word ***recover*** means to get better after being sick or hurt.
> The word ***re-cover*** means to put a new cover on something.

(See *Easy-to-Learn English Grammar and Punctuation, Part 2 of 2,* for more rules and details on *hyphens.*)

■ ■ ■

Hyphen Exercise

19A. Insert a hyphen where needed.

Example:
Question: Rita lives on Sixty Fourth Street.
Answer: Rita lives on Sixty-Fourth Street.

1. My babysitter loves sun dried tomatoes.
2. First, we will teach you a user friendly program.
3. To get a job, you must be eighteen years old.
4. Most of our twelve year old students are good readers.
5. A middle aged man was standing at the bus stop.
6. Some people are very narrow minded.
7. Sarah is a hard working girl.
8. Until the nineteen seventies, children spent a lot of time playing outdoors with their friends.
9. One fourth of the class was absent one day before the exam.
10. We had to take the stairs from his seventh floor apartment.

■ ■ ■

20. Dash (—)

Writers use dashes to give special importance to the words separated by the dash from the rest of the sentence. Sometimes, instead of a comma, semicolon, colon, and parentheses, the dash is used for these reasons:

1. To add extra information or emphasis in the sentence
   ⊳ Every year—around Christmas and New Year—we take one month's vacation.
     (dashes replace comma or parentheses)

   ⊳ My father—an intelligent, hardworking, and a very caring person—is my role model.
     (dashes add emphasis to an expression that has commas)

   ⊳ A very close friend—from my college days—is visiting me this summer.
     (dashes replace comma or parentheses)

2. To point to a list before or after the sentence—the dash replaces the colon in the following examples.
   ⊳ My mother asked me to make an after-school routine—eat a snack, play outdoors, do home-work, have dinner with family, watch my favorite show, take a bath, and go to bed by 9:00 p.m.
   ⊳ Plates, cups, cake, snacks, juice, decorations—we need all these by 5:00 p.m. for her surprise birthday party.

3. An **em** dash can be used to separate an expression that is not needed, especially when the expression has its own internal punctuation. The dashes replace parentheses in the following examples.
   ⊳ I'm ordering a vegetable pizza—with green peppers, onions, olives, and mushrooms—for dinner.
   ⊳ The car mechanic says that the car is in perfect running condition—he has checked the brakes and engine—and we can pick it up anytime.

4. To show a sudden change in thoughts, tone, or grammatical structure of the sentence.
   ⊳ Let me explain this math problem to you—did you hear the knock on the door?
   ⊳ I could not sleep till 6:00 a.m.—was it the coffee or the medicine I took?—so I'm very tired and sleepy now.
   ⊳ If I could change some things—never mind.

5. To show a pause or unfinished sentence in a dialogue.

> ⟩ "Mini, don't shut the door, or—." But Mini shut the door and got locked inside. Her mother used keys to open the door.

(See *Easy-to-Learn English Grammar and Punctuation, Part 2 of 2,* for more details on *dashes.*

■ ■ ■

Dash Exercise

> **20 A.** Insert a dash where needed.

1. Preparing well for the exam many times but not always helps to score well.
2. Please book a family restaurant a quiet, nonsmoking place with a children's play area to celebrate Sara's birthday.
3. I have ordered a long beautiful blue dress with lace embroidery and beads for the wedding.
4. When we were taking pictures by the Great Wall of China oh, let me see this text message.
5. My purse that was stolen had these important items $500 cash, eyeglasses, two credit cards, driver's license, and my passport.
6. I would like to hire Ali as the film director he is the best director and he had said that he would like to work with me.
7. "Quickly take the glass bowl from his hand or" shouted mother, but the baby threw it, and the bowl broke.

■ ■ ■

21. Parentheses ( )

Use parentheses in a sentence to include examples, facts, explanation, or any information that is not part of the main idea of the sentence. The expression in parentheses interrupts the text but gives helpful information. Generally, brackets [ ] are used if the writer adds information within a quote, and parentheses ( ) are used in unquoted text.

1. Use parentheses to show information that is less important than the rest of the sentence.
    ▷ Professor Maya Robinson (our college chemistry teacher) is on Facebook.
    ▷ The homework that you have (exercises 8 and 9) will help you prepare for tomorrow's test.

2. Use parentheses to include extra information.
    ▷ My dog barked at their rabbit. (My neighbor's white and fluffy pet.)
    ▷ We bought a new house in Lakewood (395 Central Street).
    ▷ You can take an English online exam on our website. (www.Englishexam.com)
    ▷ Before you use this machine, read the safety instructions in the manual (pages 15–19).

3. Use parentheses to make a sentence more interesting.
    ▷ For the celebration, they also invited her aunt Nancy (she's nosy and wicked) who started a fight.
    ▷ We are working with computer professionals from *PowerCom*. (The company has geniuses.)

4. Use parentheses to set off letters and numbers of items on a list.
    ▷ During their nature walk, the children made these observations: (1) some turtles sat on a log (2); a white rabbit hopped away; (3) two squirrels ran up a tree; (4) birds sat on a roof; and (5) bugs crawled in some places.
    ▷ We should not go swimming for these reasons: (a) it is extremely windy; (b) the water is very cold; (c) it is high tide; and (d) there is no lifeguard.

NOTE: In the United States, this symbol ( ) is parentheses and this [ ] is brackets.
In many countries outside the United States, this symbol ( ) is a pair of round brackets, and this [ ] is a pair of square brackets. The general term for both punctuation signs is brackets.

(See *Easy-to-Learn English Grammar and Punctuation Part 2 of 2*, for more details on parentheses.)

■ ■ ■

Parentheses Exercise

> **1.** Insert the appropriate expression with parentheses in each of the sentences below:

(a) a family friend; (b) it's poisonous; (c) a cruel woman; (d) do you remember her?; or (e) number 202-303-4004.

1. He brought a plant from another country.
2. If you need help, please call me on my phone.
3. Dr. Patrick D'Souza is giving a lecture on depression.
4. The boy's aunt has been staying with them for years.
5. My friend Aisha Patel is migrating to the United States.

■ ■ ■

22. Brackets [ ]

1. Use brackets to separate your own words, phrases, correction, explanation, or opinion within a direct quotation. Generally, brackets [ ] are used within a quote and parentheses ( ) are used in unquoted text.

   ▷ "In 1932 she [Amelia Earhart] became the first woman to fly across the Atlantic Ocean alone," said the museum guide.

   ▷ "Getting [a good night's] sleep before the exam will help you focus and remember easily the next day," the professor told her class.

   ▷ "As a result of late-night partying [the players attended three parties per night], our team lost all five games," the coach complained.

(See *Easy-to-Learn English Grammar and Punctuation Part 2 of 2,* for more rules and details on brackets.)

■ ■ ■

Brackets Exercise

22A. Insert the appropriate expression with brackets in each of the sentences below.

(a) she hits and locks up the boy; (b) she bought expensive clothes; (c) he had lot of homework; (d) coriander; (e) George Washington

1. "The leaves of this herb are used as a garnish in Latin American, Indian, and Chinese dishes," the teacher explained.
2. "Emma finished her monthly pocket money in two days and wants to borrow some from me."
3. "He was the first president of the United States of America."
4. "The boy's aunt is cruel and we want to make sure the boy stays only with his parents and not with the aunt."
5. He could not go out to play, so he is very upset.

■ ■ ■

23. Ellipsis (…)

An ellipsis mark has three dots with spaces between them (**…**). An ellipsis is primarily used to show that a part of the quote has been left out. Also, in quotations, sometimes an ellipsis is used in place of a dash to show a pause, confusion, or unfinished statement.

(See also "Interjections" and rule number 5 in "Dash" for unfinished statements and pauses.)

When you quote someone but leave out some words, use an ellipsis to show that some words or sentences from the quote are missing. Depending on which part of the quote is left out, you may have to add one more period or some other punctuation.

1. When words in the middle of a sentence are missing, replace with ellipsis only.
   - **Original quote:** Mona Johnson will not play in today's match, as she is not physically fit.
   - **Shorter quote:** "Mona Johnson**…**is not physically fit."

2. When words or sentences from the passage are missing, replace with ellipsis only.
   - **Original quote:** "Mona Johnson, the tallest basketball player in our team, needs a surgery for her arm and few weeks of physical therapy after that. She will not play in today's match, as she is not physically fit. She is likely to play in the next season."
   - **Shorter quote:** "Mona Johnson**…**is likely to play in the next season."

3. Use an ellipsis and a period together if you delete one or more complete sentences and if there is at least one complete sentence on either side of the period and ellipsis (four dots).
   - **Original quote:** "Mona Johnson, the tallest basketball player in our team, needs a surgery for her arm and few weeks of physical therapy after that. She will not play in today's match, as she is not physically fit. She is likely to play in the next season."
   - **Shorter quote:** "Mona Johnson**…**needs a surgery for her arm and few weeks of physical therapy after that**….** She is likely to play in the next season."

4. If you delete one or more lines of poetry (or paragraph of text), show the omission with one line of spaced periods.
   - "Ferry me across the water,
     Do, boatman, do."

     . . . .
     I'll ferry you."
     (Christina Rossetti)

5. Use ellipses to show hesitation or confusion.
   - "We can…er…buy this expensive dress, but…er…will she like it?" he asked.

(See *Easy-to-Learn English Grammar and Punctuation Part 2 of 2,* for more rules on ellipsis.)

■ ■ ■

24. Slash (/)

1. A slash is used to separate two choices. Note that there is no space before or after the slash.
   - We had **true/false** questions for our exams.
   - Mark **right/wrong** by the sentences below.
2. A slash is used between poetry lines if you write in text format. Leave a space before and after the slash.
   - Baa, baa, black sheep / Have you any wool? / Yes sir, yes sir, three bags full.

3. Slashes are used in other situations, such as a URL address.
   - http://www.poetryfoundation.org/poem/176321
   - http://www.ask.com/web

■ ■ ■

25. *Italics and* <u>Underlining</u>

For handwritten text, underline titles of long creative works such as books, films, and newspapers. In printed material, instead of underlining, use italics for such titles. To write in italics font means to slant the letters, which can be done in any word processing program (though the menu items or keystrokes to do this can vary from program to program.

NOTE:

Use quotation marks for titles of short works; for example, headline of a magazine article: "The Modern Ship."

Names of religious books and legal documents are not italicized.

Underline or Italicize names of the following:

1. Books
   ▷ I'm reading *The Good Earth* by Pearl S. Buck. **OR**
   ▷ I'm reading <u>The Good Earth</u> by Pearl S. Buck. (handwriting only)

2. Magazines and pamphlets

   ▷ I read an interesting article in the *Popular Science* magazine. **OR**
   ▷ I read an interesting article in the <u>Popular Science</u> magazine. (handwriting only)

3. Newspapers

   ▷ *The Washington Post* is on the dining table.   **OR**
   ▷ <u>The Washington Post</u> is on the dining table. (handwriting only)

4. Poems, plays, and published speeches
   ▷ We acted out the poem *Lord Ullin's Daughter* by Thomas Campbell. **OR**
   ▷ We acted out the poem <u>Lord Ullin's Daughter</u> by Thomas Campbell. (handwriting only)

5. Films, radio and television shows (the titles of series but not the titles of episodes), DVDs, CDs, and other media

   ▷ The movie *Titanic* attracted large crowds in many countries. **OR**
   ▷ The movie <u>Titanic</u> attracted large crowds in many countries. (handwriting only)

    ▷ Do you watch the television show *Good Morning America?* **OR**

    ▷ Do you watch the television show <u>Good Morning America?</u> (handwriting only)

6.   Musical works and visual art

    ▷ Have you heard Beethoven's *Symphony No. 9 in D Minor?*   **OR**

    ▷ Have you heard Beethoven's <u>Symphony No. 9 in D Minor</u>? (handwriting only)

    ▷ Leonardo da Vinci's popular paintings are *Last Supper* and *Mona Lisa.* **OR**

    ▷ Leonardo da Vinci's popular paintings are <u>Last Supper</u> and <u>Mona Lisa.</u> (handwriting only)

(See *Easy-to-Learn English Grammar and Punctuation Part 2 of 2,* for more rules on italics and underlining.)

■ ■ ■

Italics and Underlining Exercise

25A. Underline or put in quotations the appropriate titles below.

1. My son loves the book Animal Homes.
2. Voyager 2 is the first spacecraft to fly by the planet Uranus.
3. The Andaman Express, a long-distance express train in India, runs between Chennai and Jammu.
4. Do you have a copy of Newsweek?
5. I'm reading an article titled What We Know About the Universe.
6. Let's watch the television show America's Funniest Home Videos.

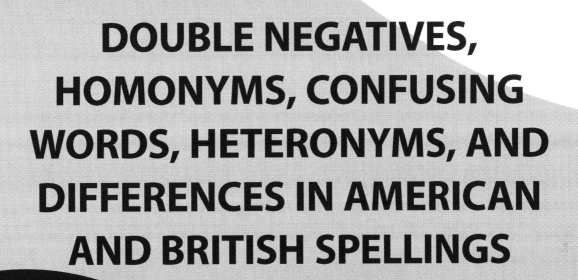

DOUBLE NEGATIVES, HOMONYMS, CONFUSING WORDS, HETERONYMS, AND DIFFERENCES IN AMERICAN AND BRITISH SPELLINGS

26. Double Negatives

A double negative means a sentence has two negative (or **<u>no</u>**) words. Sometimes, people use sentences with two negatives to express one negative meaning; however, two negatives give a positive meaning. If we want to express one negative meaning, only one negative word should be used.

For example, if the speaker wants to say that she does not want any advice, and if she says "I don't need no advice," she actually expresses the meaning that she wants advice.
In the examples below, the two negatives are underlined.

⊳	I <u>don't</u> need <u>no</u> advice.	**Wrong** (two negatives)
⊳	I **don't** need any advice.	**Correct** (one negative)
⊳	I need **no** advice.	**Correct** (one negative)
⊳	You <u>haven't</u> got <u>no</u> manners.	**Wrong**
⊳	You <u>ain't</u> got <u>no</u> manners. (ain't=slang)	**Wrong**
⊳	You **haven't** got any manners.	**Correct**
⊳	You have **no** manners.	**Correct**
⊳	You **don't** have any manners.	**Correct**

See page 145 for nonstandard contractions such as *ain't*, in English slang.

⊳	He <u>didn't</u> shout at <u>nobody.</u>	**Wrong**
⊳	He **didn't** shout at anybody.	**Correct**
⊳	He shouted at **nobody.**	**Correct**
⊳	We <u>aren't</u> serving <u>no</u> more drinks.	**Wrong**
⊳	We **aren't** serving any more drinks.	**Correct**
⊳	We are serving **no** more drinks.	**Correct**

In a sentence when you use the word *not* or a contraction that has *not* (*don't, haven't, didn't, aren't,* etc.), check to see if there are any more negative words. Accordingly, change the other negative word to a positive word. For example, you can change *no* to *any, nobody* to *anybody*, and *no more* to *anymore*.

The words **scarcely, hardly,** and **barely** have a negative meaning and are used to say only that something is true or possible. Therefore, avoid using another negative word with these words. **Scarcely, hardly,** and **barely** are often used between the helping verb (*can, could, have, be,* etc.) and the main verb.

> ▸   I can <u>scarcely</u> <u>not</u> understand what is going on.   **Wrong** (two negatives)
> ▸   I can **scarcely** understand what is going on.   **Correct**
>
> ▸   There is <u>hardly</u> <u>no</u> ice cream left.   **Wrong**
> ▸   There is **hardly** any ice cream left.   **Correct**
>
> ▸   They could <u>barely</u> <u>not</u> read nor write.   **Wrong**
> ▸   They could **barely** read or write.   **Correct**

■ ■ ■

27. Homonyms or Homophones
(Words that Sound Alike)

Homonyms, or **homophones**, are words that sound alike but have different spellings and meanings. Some of the listed words below may have many more meanings, so refer to the dictionary to find out more about these words. (The list is alphabetical.)

1. **all ready**	prepared
2. **already**	by this or that time
3. **allowed**	to give permission to or for
4. **aloud**	in a voice that other people can hear
5. **ate**	past tense of eat
6. **eight**	a number
7. **aunt**	the sister of your father or mother; the wife of your uncle
8. **ant**	a small insect
9. **bear**	a wild animal with thick fur (noun), to carry (verb)
10. **bare**	not covered
11. **beau** (pronounced *bo*)	boyfriend
12. **bow** (pronounced *bo*)	a wood strip bent by strings to shoot arrows
13. **bough** (pronounced *bau*)	branch of a tree
14. **bow** (pronounced *bau*)	to bend your head forwards and downwards as a sign of respect
15. **blue**	a color
16. **blew**	past of blow; something that was in motion
17. **board**	a flat piece of material (noun); to get on a bus, train, plane, etc. (verb)
18. **bored**	uninterested

19. **born**	brought to life
20. **borne**	carried
21. **break**	to be damaged and separated into two or more parts, as a result of force (verb); recess (noun)
22. **brake**	a device for stopping
23. **bury**	to put in the ground and cover with earth
24. **berry**	a small juicy fruit
25. **by**	close to or next to (someone or something)
26. **buy**	to pay and get something
27. **capitol**	building in Washington DC where the US Congress meets
28. **capital**	a city which is the official seat of the government; highly important; uppercase letter
29. **coarse**	rough in texture; large particles
30. **course**	direction; path; series of lessons
31. **dear**	loved by somebody
32. **deer**	an animal with long legs
33. **die**	to stop living
34. **dye**	to change the color of something
35. **fair**	to treat people equally; large; light in complexion
36. **fare**	money paid for travel; a taxi passenger; food
37. **feat**	work that needs skill, strength, or courage
38. **feet**	lowest part of legs (plural of foot)
39. **flour**	powder from grain
40. **flower**	a part of plant
41. **flu**	a bad cold; an infection
42. **flew**	moved through air (past tense of fly)
43. **forth**	onward or outward in place or space
44. **fourth**	next after the third

45. **heal**	to become healthy again
46. **heel**	back part of the foot to below the ankle
47. **he'll**	he will
48. **hear**	to be aware of sound through ears
49. **here**	in this place; at this point in time
50. **heard**	past tense of hear
51. **herd**	a group of same type of animals
52. **hole**	an opening through something
53. **whole**	complete; full amount
54. **I**	a letter in the alphabet; subject pronoun
55. **eye**	organs used to see
56. **its**	possessive pronoun to show belonging
57. **it's**	contraction of **it is**
58. **knead**	to press and stretch dough
59. **kneed**	to hit or push with one's knee
60. **need**	to require something important
61. **lessen**	to make smaller or less
62. **lesson**	learning material or class; an experience
63. **loan**	money borrowed
64. **lone**	being alone
65. **mail**	letters etc. sent and delivered by the post office
66. **male**	from the masculine gender
67. **main**	largest; most important of its kind
68. **mane**	long hair on the neck of a horse or a lion
69. **meet**	to come together
70. **meat**	flesh of animals used as food

71. **new**	recent; not used before
72. **knew**	past tense of know; to have information
73. **not**	used to express negation
74. **knot**	a join made by tying two pieces
75. **one**	the number one
76. **won**	to finish first in a competition
77. **our**	possessive pronoun
78. **hour**	60 minutes
79. **pail**	bucket
80. **pale**	not bright
81. **passed**	past tense of pass; to achieve the required standard; to move by someone or something; handed to
82. **past**	gone by in time; before the present
83. **peace**	calm; quiet; no war
84. **piece**	section
85. **pear**	a fruit
86. **pair**	two similar things matched to use together
87. **pare**	to cut off outer layer
88. **plain**	clear; simple
89. **plane**	airplane; flat surface
90. **pray**	to offer a prayer
91. **prey**	an animal, etc. hunted, killed and eaten by another animal
92. **principal**	main; important; head of school
93. **principle**	a moral rule or strong belief
94. **reign**	the period during which a king, etc. rules
95. **rein**	method to control, check, or direct; a strap around a horse's bridle
96. **rain**	water that falls from the sky

97. **right** 98. **write**	true; correct; morally good; normal make lectures or words on a surface
99. **road** 100. **rode**	a long paved surface; a way (past tense of ride) carried on the back of an animal or inside a vehicle
101. **roll** 102. **role**	long piece of anything wrapped around itself proper function; part played by an actor
103. **sale** 104. **sail**	the act of selling something; giving something for money to travel on water using a boat or ship
105. **scene** 106. **seen**	place where something happens past tense of see
107. **sea** 108. **see**	salt water that covers most of the earth's surface to be aware of something using eyes
109. **sent** 110. **cent** 111. **scent**	past tense of send; to give to someone across a distance 100th part of the main unit of money (euro or dollar) a pleasant smell
112. **so** 113. **sew**	very; also; (conjunction) to stitch
114. **soar** 115. **sore**	to fly at a great height a wound; hurt
116. **some** 117. **sum**	few; approximately; a portion an amount; a sum total; arithmetic problem
118. **son** 119. **sun**	male child the star that gives us light and heat and is the central object of our solar system
120. **stair** 121. **stare**	steps between floors to look at someone or something for a long time without moving your eyes

122. **stationary**	standing still; not moving
123. **stationery**	writing materials
124. **steal**	to take something that is not yours in a wrong or illegal way
125. **steel**	a strong, hard metal of iron and carbon
126. **strait**	a water passage that connects two large bodies of water
127. **straight**	direct; without a bend; vertical; open and frank
128. **tale**	a story
129. **tail**	part of an animal, fish, or bird's body
130. **than**	used to compare two things, people, situations, etc.
131. **then**	at a particular time; next
132. **their**	(possessive pronoun) belonging to them
133. **there**	at that place; that state
134. **they're**	they are
135. **threw**	(past tense of throw) sent something through the air
136. **through**	from one point to another
137. **to**	in the direction of something; towards something
138. **too**	also; as well; very
139. **two**	a number
140. **wait**	to stay in a place until an expected event
141. **weight**	the heaviness of a person or thing
142. **waste**	not used properly
143. **waist**	middle part of the body between the hips and chest
144. **way**	road; a style or method of doing something
145. **weigh**	to measure how heavy a person, animal, or thing is
146. **weak**	not firm or strong
147. **week**	seven days in a row
148. **wear**	have clothes on the body
149. **where**	at what place

150. **weather**	outside conditions such as air, rain, clouds, snow, etc.
151. **whether**	which one of the two
152. **which**	one from a group
153. **witch**	a woman who practices black magic
154. **who's**	who is; who has
155. **whose**	possessive pronoun of who
156. **wood**	hard material that forms the trunk and branches of a tree
157. **would**	past tense of will
158. **your**	belonging to you
159. **you're**	you are

■ ■ ■

28. Confusing Words

The list below has words that may seem similar, but they have different spellings, meanings, and pronunciations. The English language has many more such confusing words, so when you are in doubt, always check your dictionary to use the correct word.

1. **accept**	to receive or take
2. **except**	other than; not including
3. **accent**	a way of pronouncing words; to give special attention to
4. **ascent**	upward slope or movement
5. **affect**	to act on; produce an effect or change
6. **effect**	result
7. **be**	to exist; to be present; the verb <u>be</u>
8. **bee**	an insect
9. **been**	past participle of <u>be</u>
10. **bin**	a box or container
11. **coma**	to be in an unconscious state for a long time
12. **comma (,)**	a punctuation mark
13. **conscience**	the part of your mind that tells whether your actions are right or wrong
14. **conscious**	aware of one's surroundings
15. **cooperation**	working together with a shared purpose
16. **corporation**	company, business, or organization
17. **deceased**	no longer living; dead
18. **diseased**	illness

19. **decent**	good standard or quality
20. **descent**	downward slope or movement
21. **dessert**	sweet eaten at the end of a meal
22. **desert**	large land areas of sand with very little water
23. **emigrate**	to leave a country to live somewhere else
24. **immigrate**	to come to a country to live
25. **eminent**	honored; well-known
26. **imminent**	ready to take place
27. **farther**	to a far distance, place, or time
28. **further**	to a great degree or extent; to a far distance, place, or time
29. **finally**	happening as a result; coming at the end
30. **finely**	in a fine manner
31. **human**	relating to people
32. **humane**	having compassion, sympathy, or consideration for humans or animals
33. **latter**	relating to the end of a process, activity, series, life, etc.
34. **later**	after a given time or stage
35. **lay**	to put or set down
36. **lie** (1)	to be or to stay at rest
37. **lie** (2)	to make an untrue statement
38. **loose**	not tight
39. **lose** (1)	unable to find
40. **lose** (2)	fail to win
41. **lovable**	easy to love; having qualities that deserve love
42. **loving**	feeling or showing love
43. **personal**	relating to a particular person
44. **personnel**	people working for a company or organization
45. **quiet**	making very little or no noise
46. **quite**	completely; really; to a large extent

47. **sweet**	taste of sugar, honey, etc.
48. **suite**	set of connected rooms in a hotel
49. **then**	particular time in the past or future; next; as a result
50. **than**	used for comparing
51. **thorough**	completely and carefully
52. **through**	from one side / end to another
53. **umpire**	person appointed to give decisions in sports events
54. **empire**	regions ruled by one ruler or one government; a very large business owned by one person or company
55. **understandable**	easy to understand; seem normal and reasonable
56. **understanding**	the ability to understand; to have knowledge; a way in which somebody understands something

■ ■ ■

29. Heteronyms (Homographs)

Heteronyms, or **homographs,** are words that have the same spelling but different meanings and pronunciations. In the pronunciation column below, note the difference in how the syllables are stressed for the same word. This is not a complete list of heteronyms.

Word	Pronunciation	Meaning
1. **August** (noun)	AW-ghust	the eighth month of the year
2. **august** (adjective)	aw-GUHST	majestic dignity, grandeur, eminent
3. **bass** (noun)	bas	type of fish
4. **bass** (adjective)	beys	deep in tone, of low sound or pitch
5. **bow** (noun)	bo (like so)	a wood strip bent by strings to shoot arrows
6. **bow** (verb)	bau (like cow)	to bend your head forwards and downwards as a sign of respect
7. **conduct** (noun)	KON-duhkt	the way a person behaves
8. **conduct** (verb)	kuhn-DUHKT	to guide, lead, direct, or do an activity
9. **content** (noun)	KON-tent	topic or matter contained
10. **content** (adjective)	kuhn-TENT	pleased and satisfied
11. **lead** (noun)	led	heavy metal
12. **lead** (verb)	leed	to guide, to go before
13. **minute** (noun)	MIN-it	sixty seconds
14. **minute** (adjective)	mahy-NYOOT	extremely small in size
15. **produce** (noun)	PROH-dyoos	vegetables and fruits collectively, offspring of an animal
16. **produce** (verb)	pruh-DYOOS	to make, give rise to

17. **re-creation** (noun)	ree-kree-EY-shuhn	to create something anew
18. **recreation** (noun)	REK-ree-EY-shuhn	pastime, relaxation and enjoyment
19. **refuse** (noun)	REF-yoos	rubbish, trash, garbage
20. **refuse** (verb)	ri-FYOOZ	to decline to give, to deny (a request, demand, etc.)
21. **row** (noun, verb)	roh (like *so*)	a line of persons or things; to move a vessel forward
22. **row** (noun)	rou (like *cow*)	a noisy quarrel
23. **résumé** (noun)	REZ-yoo-mey, rez-oo-MEY	a document of personal, educational, and professional qualifications
24. **resume** (verb)	ri-ZYOOM	to take up again
25. **tear** (noun)	tee-er	fluid that flows from the eye
26. **tear** (verb)	tair (like *air*)	to pull apart by force, to rip
27. **wind** (noun)	wind	air that moves quickly
28. **wind** (verb)	wahynd (like *kind*)	to change direction, turn, to coil or twine about something
29. **wound** (noun)	woond	an injury or hurt
30. **wound** (verb)	WOWnd	coiled up

■ ■ ■

30. Differences in American and British Spellings

Outside the United States of America, most English speakers are used to British spellings and pronunciations. The main differences in spellings are listed below.

British	North American
1. aerogramme, kilogramme, programme	1. aerogram, kilogram, program
2. theatre, calibre, centre, fibre, litre, metre	2. theater, caliber, center, fiber, liter, meter
3. analyse, apologise, criticise, emphasise, organise, paralyse, realise, recognise	3. analyze, apologize, criticize, emphasize, organize, paralyze, realize, recognize
4. behaviour, colour, neighbour, favour, honour, humour, labour, parlour, rumour,	4. behavior, color, neighbor, favor, honor, humor, labor, parlor, rumor,
5. cancelled, dialled, labelled, quarrelled travelled	5. canceled, dialed, labeled, quarreled, traveled
6. cancelling, dialling, labelling, quarrelling, travelling	6. canceling, dialing, labeling, quarreling, traveling
7. jeweller, traveller	7. jeweler, traveler
8. enrol, enthral, fulfil	8. enroll, enthrall, fulfill
9. defence, licence	9. defense, license
10. judgement	10. judgment

Spelling differences in some other words

British	North American
1. ageing	1. aging
2. aluminium	2. aluminum
3. anaemia / anaemic	3. anemia / anemic
4. anaesthesia	4. anesthesia
5. axe	5. ax
6. caesarean	6. cesarean
7. cheque / chequebook	7. check /checkbook
8. chilli	8. chili
9. diarrhoea	9. diarrhea
10. gaol / jail	10. jail
11. moustache	11. mustache
12. omelette	12. omelet /omelette
13. practise (verb)	13. practise / practice (verbs)
14. pyjama / pyjamas	14. pajama /pajamas
15. storey /storeys	15. story /stories / storeys
16. tyre /tyres	16. tire / tires
17. woollen	17. woolen

■ ■ ■

Answers Section

From the Title Page

Find out what is wrong with this sentence, **and** learn a lot more in this **easy-to-use** guide to English grammar and punctuation!

(Explanation: Use a comma when a coordinating conjunction joins two independent clauses.
Also, use a hyphen to join adjectives when they come before a noun *as one unit* and modify that noun.)

---

1. Nouns

1A:

1. proper 2. proper 3. common 4. common (collective) 5. proper 6. common (compound) 7. common 8. abstract 9. abstract 10. common (compound) 11. common (collective) 12. proper 13. proper 14. proper

1B:

Sentences	Proper	Common
1. <u>India</u> is a <u>country</u>.	India	country
2. <u>People</u> speak different <u>languages</u>.		people, languages
3. My <u>friend</u>, <u>Adam</u>, knows the <u>truth</u>.	Adam	friend, truth
4. The <u>Taj Mahal</u> is beautiful.	Taj Mahal	
5. We must work for <u>peace</u>.		peace
6. We must have <u>patience</u> all the <u>time</u>.		patience, time
7. The <u>sun</u> gives us <u>light</u> and <u>heat</u>.		sun, light, heat
8. The <u>Nile River</u> is long.	Nile River	
9. Our <u>team</u> won the <u>game</u>.		team, game
10. The <u>Pacific Ocean</u> is the largest <u>ocean</u>.	Pacific Ocean	ocean

1C:

1. concrete 2. concrete 3. abstract 4. abstract 5. concrete 6. concrete 7. abstract 8. abstract 9. concrete 10. concrete

1D:

1. The boy's money is on the desk.
2. The dancers' costumes are beautiful. / The dancer's costumes are beautiful.
3. India's population is over one billion.
4. The girls' racquets are in the locker. / The girl's racquets are in the locker.
5. My mother's purse is brown.

2. Pronouns

2A:

1. they 2. they 3. he 4. she 5. it 6. they 7. they 8. we 9. they 10. we

2B:

1. we 2. she, he 3. his 4. her 5. they 6. we 7. its 8. she, them 9. it 10. they

2C:

1. I didn't sell <u>it</u> to Tim. 2. My sister will babysit <u>them</u>. 3. They are giving <u>it</u> to us.
4. Seema was talking with <u>him.</u> 5. We cannot do without <u>it.</u>

2D:

1. intensive, reflexive 2. intensive, reflexive 3. intensive 4. reflexive 5. intensive 6. reflexive 7. reflexive 8. intensive 9. reflexive 10. reflexive 11. reflexive 12. reflexive 13. intensive 14. reflexive 15. intensive 16. intensive 17. intensive 18. intensive 19. intensive 20. reflexive

2E:

1. who 2. whose 3. our 4. us 5. these, those 6. that 7. you 8. whoever 9. their, ours 10. whom 11. our / your 12. us / me 13. whoever 14. neither / someone 15. whom 16. no one 17. your, their 18. this, that 19. theirs 20. its 21. whom (**who** is also used, but **whom** is correct) 22. she 23. myself 24. whomever 25. both 26. most / few 27. whichever 28. most 29. I 30. she

2F:

1. She and I had a fight. 2. You and she will work tomorrow. 3. We had invited him to meet with the students. 4. Those dirty clothes are hers. 5. The teacher wrote to them. 6. Are you going to eat these chips? 7. We asked for directions, but no one knew. 8. The manager told two workers and me not to bring food. 9. She and I have not met for many days. 10. These eggs are rotten.

2G:

1.   They 2. we 3. They 4. She 5. We 6. He 7. She 8. We

3. Verbs

3A:

1.   are / were/ will be 2. was 3. was 4. are / will be 5. is / was 6. are / were /will be 7. will be

3B:

1.   a, d. 2. b, c 3. a, b, d 4. a, b, c, 5. c 6. b, d 7. b, c, d 8. c, d 9. a 10. c, d

3C:

1.   cut, 2. saw, 3. broke, 4. wore, 5. shook, 6. did, 7. had, 8. came, 9. did, 10. do

3D:

Today I <u>am</u>. (be) home.

I **am**(be) at my desk, and I **am writing** (write) this letter to you.

How **are**be) you, and how **is** (be) your family?

These days my office **starts** (start) at 11:00 a.m.

I **come** (come) home at 7:00 p.m.

We **have** (have) lot of work in the office.

Yesterday, I **wanted** (want) to go to see the new movie, but I could not. We **will go**(go) next Saturday.

Last July, I **had** (have) fun with you when we **went** (go) to eat at the restaurant.

I also **enjoyed** (enjoy) when you **came** (come) to visit me at my place.

Yesterday, my friend, Tina, **asked** (ask) me to **join** (join) her at a restaurant for dinner.

We **ate** (eat) at the Taj Mahal restaurant.

We also **watched** (watch) a movie on TV. Then we **listened** (listen) to some songs.

After that, we **went** (go) for a walk. But it **started** (start) to rain.

We **were**(be) all wet by the time we **reached** (reach) home.

It **was raining** (rain) for four hours.

"Why **did** (do) you not take your umbrellas?" **asked** (ask) my brother?

Now, I have to go to **pick** (pick) up my daughter from school.

She **stays** (stay) at the day-care after school.

She **likes** (like) to eat after she **comes** (come) home. I **made** (make) her some snacks.

I **hope** (hope) to hear from you soon. So, please **write** (write) soon.

3E:

	Main verb	Type	Tense	Basic word
1	corrected	regular	simple past	correct
2.	drank	irregular	simple past	drink
3.	helping	regular	present continuous	help
4.	became	irregular	simple past	become
5.	began	irregular	simple past	begin
6.	dropped	regular	simple past	drop
7.	learning	regular	present continuous	learn
8.	saw	irregular	simple past	see
9.	found	irregular	simple past	find
10.	had	irregular	simple past	have

3F:

1. a, b 2.a, b, d 3. a, b 4.b, c 5.a, d 6.a, b, c, d 7.d 8.a, b (past tense), c 9. a, b 10. b

4. Adjectives

4A:

1. A <u>huge</u> elephant just passed this way.
2. This hotel is <u>dirty</u>.
3. Do you have some <u>ice-cold</u> drinking water?
4. Mr. Smith is our <u>French</u> teacher.
5. This is a <u>small</u> bedroom. Do you have anything <u>bigger</u>?
6. I do not remember a lot about the exam, but it was <u>tough.</u>
7. My phone is <u>red</u> and hers is <u>black</u>.
8. Sameer washed his car. His car is <u>clean</u>.

4B:

clean X <u>dirty,</u> tall X <u>short,</u> dull X <u>bright or sharp</u>, high X <u>low,</u> easy X <u>hard or difficult</u>
big X <u>small</u>, young X <u>old,</u> cold X <u>hot,</u> good X <u>bad,</u> happy X <u>sad,</u> pretty X <u>ugly,</u>
loud X <u>soft,</u> fast X <u>slow,</u> expensive X <u>cheap,</u> thin X <u>fat or thick,</u> selfish X <u>selfless,</u>
wise X <u>foolish,</u> kind X <u>cruel,</u> rough X <u>smooth</u>

4C:

1. The <u>lovely</u> greeting card is on <u>your</u> desk.
2. A <u>gentle</u> breeze is blowing from the east.

3. I hope you are having a <u>good</u> time.
4. Can we meet <u>next</u> week?
5. Are you taking the <u>English</u> class?
6. Those <u>brown</u> sunglasses are mine.
7. I am listening to some <u>amazing</u> music.
8. It is an <u>interesting</u> book.
9. Tina and her brother are <u>smart</u> kids.
10. I have <u>good</u> neighbors.
11. It is a <u>noisy</u> party, so I stepped out.
12. My <u>favorite</u> TV show starts at 9:00 p.m.
13. The <u>last</u> bus leaves the station at 10:00 p.m.
14. The <u>free</u> concert attracted a <u>huge</u> crowd.
15. We cannot play outside, as it is a <u>rainy</u> day.

4D:

1. interested 2. shocking 3. excited 4. wanted 5. amusing 6. tired 7. surprised 8. satisfying 9. confusing 10. enjoy

4E:

1. sweet 2. taller 3. more expensive 4. bigger 5. youngest
6. more careful 7. heaviest 8. nicer 9. later 10. better

5. Adverbs

5A:

1. dangerously 2. carefully 3. suddenly 4. quietly 5. rapidly
6. clearly 7. nervously 8. perfectly 9. badly 10. easily

5B:

1. <u>Softly</u> describes the verb <u>speaking</u>; <u>too</u> describes the adverb <u>softly</u>.
2. <u>Angrily</u> describes the verb <u>talk.</u>
3. <u>Happily</u> describes the verb phrase <u>is looking.</u>
4. <u>Quickly</u> describes the verb <u>finish.</u>
5. <u>Very</u> describes the adjective <u>good.</u>
6. <u>Somewhat</u> describes the adjective <u>careless.</u>
7. <u>Never</u> describes the verb <u>open.</u> <u>Always</u> describes the adjective <u>tight.</u>
8. <u>Extremely</u> describes the adjective <u>clever.</u>
9. <u>Slowly</u> describes the verb <u>drive.</u>
10. <u>Very</u> describes the adjective <u>sleepy.</u>

5C:

1. First 2. away 3. Once 4. sadly 5. completely 6. frequently 7. almost 8. well 9. always 10. quite

5D:

1. <u>fast</u> = adjective, linking verb = <u>is</u> 2. <u>quickly</u> = adverb 3. <u>beautiful</u> = adjective. Linking verb = <u>looks</u> 4. <u>fluently</u> = adverb 5. <u>neat</u> = adjective 6. <u>correctly</u> = adverb 7. <u>loud</u> = adjective 8. <u>careless</u> = adjective 9. <u>easily</u> = adverb 10. <u>clearly</u> = adverb 11. <u>regularly</u> = adverb 12. <u>slow</u> = adjective, linking verb = <u>were</u> 13. <u>nervous</u> = adjective, linking verb = <u>appeared</u> 14. <u>angrily</u> = adverb 15. <u>well</u> = adverb 16. <u>worse</u> = adjective, linking verb = <u>is</u> 17. <u>late</u> = adverb 18. <u>less</u> = adverb 19. <u>soon</u> = adverb 20. <u>far</u> = adverb

6. Prepositions

6A:

	Prepositions	Objects
1. They ran <u>between the flower beds</u>.	between	beds
2. <u>During the holidays</u>, we spend time <u>with our friends</u>.	during	holidays
	with	friends
3. <u>Outside the theater</u>, you will see food stalls.	outside	theater
4. <u>Past the garage</u>, the road turns right <u>to the school</u>.	past	garage
	to	school
5. <u>In spite of our exams</u>, we watched the entire movie.	in spite of	exams
6. All students took part <u>in sports</u>.	in	sports
7. The English book is <u>next to the clock</u> <u>on the shelf</u>.	next	clock
	on	shelf
8. The woman knocked <u>on the door</u> and went <u>behind the house</u>.	on	door
	behind	house
9. Please go <u>up the stairs</u> <u>to the fourth floor</u>.	up	stairs
	to	floor
10. The actor walked <u>on to the stage</u> and gave a speech.	on	stage

6B: Any appropriate preposition or compound preposition is correct. Here are some choices.

1. onto, over 2. across, in front of, behind, around, near, away from 3. under, behind, on, in front of, across 4. next 5. up, down, across, along, around 6. within, after, to 7. along, by, in, during 8. instead of

6C:

Prepositional phrases underlined	Subject and verb
1. My teacher gave textbooks <u>to everyone</u>.	My teacher gave textbooks.
2. The bus driver drove away <u>without picking up all. the students</u>.	The bus driver drove away.
3. You must arrive ten minutes <u>before tests and exams</u>.	You must arrive.
4. There are many other stars <u>besides the sun</u>.	There are many other stars.
5. Our train passed <u>through three tunnels</u>.	Our train passed.

7. Conjunctions

7A:

1. The little girl is playing**, and** her brother is sleeping.
2. I ran to catch the bus**, but** I still missed it.
3. We had cleaned the house before they came**, but** the children made it untidy again.
4. Many dresses were on sale**, yet** we did not buy any.
5. We returned home from the kite-flying contest**,** celebrated**, and** ate snacks.
6. Is your exam tomorrow **or** the day after tomorrow?
7. Tina enjoys watching TV serials **and** movies **but** dislikes watching sports.
8. The doctor's office was closed**, so** they went to see another doctor.
9. They do not have a good income**, yet** they bought the expensive jewelry anyway.
10. I will not sign this proposal**, for** I do not agree with your idea.

7B:

1. neither, nor 2. Both, and 3. not only, but also 4. Either, or 5. Not, but 6. not only, but also
7. whether, or 8. whether, or 9. both, and 10. not, but

7C:

1. **<u>Unless</u> <u>you start one hour before class</u>,** 2. **<u>where</u> <u>she's hiding the birthday presents</u>?**
3. **<u>When</u> <u>we went to the shopping mall</u>,** 4. **<u>After</u> <u>buying cake at the bakery</u>,** 5. **<u>if</u> <u>we can get forty tickets for the show</u>** 6. **<u>Although</u> <u>he had an umbrella</u>,** he never used it **<u>while</u> <u>it was raining</u>.** 7. **<u>Whenever</u> <u>you get a chance</u>,** 8. **<u>as</u> soon <u>as</u> <u>I put him in the crib</u>.** 9. **<u>how</u> <u>the letter reached so late</u>.** 10. **<u>while</u> <u>surfing the Internet</u>.**

8. Interjections

8A:

Many interjections can convey the same meaning. Therefore, one sentence can have more than one correct interjection. The interjection that you have used may or may not be written here.

1. <u>Oh no!</u> or <u>Oops!</u> or <u>Oh dear!</u> I forgot to bring my phone.
2. <u>Hey!</u> or <u>Good grief!</u> or <u>Goodness!</u> That is not what I said!
3. <u>Wow!</u> or <u>Heavens!</u> or <u>Indeed,</u> what a beautiful sight!
4. <u>Hooray!</u> or <u>Yippee!</u> We won the lottery!
5. <u>Oh no!</u> or <u>What?</u> or <u>My goodness!</u> You told the supervisor that she is crazy?
6. <u>Shame!</u> or <u>Oh no!</u> or <u>Darn!</u> We cannot meet.
7. <u>Phew!</u> or <u>Oops!</u> or <u>Oh Oh!</u> or <u>Oh no!</u> My scarf flew away.
8. <u>Whoops!</u> or <u>Yikes!</u> or <u>Oh no!</u> or <u>Oh dear!</u> The roof is leaking.
9. <u>Well,</u> now, she cannot fool us anymore!
10. <u>Ouch!</u> I stubbed my toe badly.

8B:

1. Aah! So that was the trick.
2. Yippee! Schools are closing because of the stormy weather.
3. What! Share all my birthday presents with him?
4. Dude! I cannot believe it.
5. Sh! People are praying.
6. Hello, are you listening?
7. Ugh! There are earthworms everywhere.
8. So! You do plan to help out with the work.
9. Hm... the story line was good, but the acting was bad.
8. Indeed! It was a great game.

9. Articles

9A:

1. **The** traffic is quite a lot in **the** morning and evening.
2. **The** homework that I used to get in college took up all my time.
3. Did you go to **the** concert that you and your husband wanted to go to?
4. February was **the** coldest month of **the** year.
5. **The** crowd became restless when their favorite actor did not show up for a long time.
6. Continuous rain made **the** water rise in **the** river.
7. It was **an** interesting movie.
8. Have you seen **an** alligator?
9. Some brave people have visited **the** earth's South Pole.
10. She lives on Park Avenue in New York.
11. The Himalayas are nature's wonder, and **the** Taj Mahal is **a** man-made wonder.
12. We saw **the** White House, **the** Great Wall of China, and Lake Superior recently.
13. **The** river Nile empties into **the** Mediterranean Sea.
14. We will be visiting India and **the** United Kingdom.
15. The patient has high blood pressure and diabetes.
16. Why don't you play piano for us? (As a command or imperative, *play piano* is correct and does not need an article. *Play the piano* is also acceptable.)

17. They were playing baseball in **the** rain.

9B: The quantifiers you have used may be different from the quantifiers in the answers below, but if your quantifiers are appropriate, your answer is correct.

1. I gave the beggar <u>some</u> money.
2. Sprinkle <u>very little</u> salt on the popcorn.
3. Please order <u>a great deal of</u> sugar.
4. The baby will have <u>any</u> cake.
5. We have <u>plenty of</u> ice cream.
6. Please order <u>**a**</u> kilogram of sugar.
7. We have <u>**a**</u> carton of ice cream.
8. The guest will have <u>**a**</u> slice of cake.
9. We had <u>great</u> help on the trip.
10. Do you have <u>**a**</u> saltshaker?
11. The students need <u>a lot of</u> guidance.
12. I hope we can get <u>some</u> information quickly.

10. Capitalization

10 A:

1. Do, Diwali, India 2. Like, Diwali, Christmas, Ramadan Eid 3. I, English 4. We, Indians, Chinese, French, Hispanics, Americans 5. The, President of the United States 6. We, Coca-Cola 7. I, Grandma 8. The, English, H. G. Wells, 9. My, Sunday, February 10. I, American Airlines

11. Period and Capitalization

11 A:

1. Is his meeting in Jan. or Feb.?
2. Dr. Roy asked you to take one tablet at 8:00 a.m. and another at 8:00 p.m.
3. They were asking when the park will open.
4. We took sandwiches, juice, chips, and pastries for the picnic.
5. The farewell party is on Mon., Feb. 10.
6. Julius Caesar, the Roman leader, reached Britain with an army in 55 BC.
7. When are you getting your BA degree?
8. Most homes have a TV and phone these days.
9. Please cross the road at the crossing.
10. Please mail this package to Mr. S. K. Chen:
    PO Box 124
    Main St.
    NY 20453
    USA

12. Comma

12 A:

1. Mrs. Robinson is our English teacher**, and** Mr. Chopra is our music teacher.
2. Maya**,** your science teacher wants to talk with us.
3. Last Saturday**,** for example**,** the guitar player did not show up.
4. No**,** we do not like that ants are crawling around in our house.
5. We are taking a vacation in summer**,** not in winter.
6. I need textbooks for English**,** science**,** geography**,** history**,** and French.
7. Today**,** I want you to deposit the money in the bank**,** pick up the medicines from the pharmacy**,** get some groceries**,** and attend your sister's music recital.
8. He shouted**,** "Get out of here!"
9. They are playing very badly**,** aren't they?
10. "It is a great honor to play for my country**,**" he said.
11. If you can sing**,** sing.
12. Danny is a pilot; David**,** an astronaut.
13. Natasha ate fish for dinner; Katrina**,** chicken.
14. We have a trained**,** honest**,** certified technician to repair your computer.
15. The house inspectors are coming on Monday**,** 17 August 2014.
16. The marathon is on Thursday**,** May 29**,** 2015.
17. Can you find Miami**,** Florida on the map and show me?
18. Her flight**,** in fact**,** is arriving late.
19. Yesterday we had eighteen inches of snow**,** and it was really**,** really cold.
20. My English professor**,** Maryam**,** is a wonderful person.

13 and 14. Capitalization and Punctuation

13 and 14 A:

1) **O**h no**! I** forgot my homework again**.**
2) **D**id she close the door**?**
3) **W**hat a magic trick**!**
4) **W**hich dress should **I** wear**?** Blue**?** Pink**?** Red**?**
5) **S**he wants to know if you will teach the class today**.**
6) **D**aisy worked on weekends**.**
7) **W**ho is going to help us**? M**aria**? A**mar**?** Rita**?**
8) **H**e is offering you a job, isn't he**?**
9) **S**tay calm and just correct the mistakes**.**
10) **R**un**!** The house is full of smoke**!**

15. Apostrophe and Contractions

15 A.

1. Ms. Roy's purse is in the staff room.
2. The nurses' uniforms are in the changing room. (more than one nurse) **OR**

The nurse's uniforms are in the changing room. (One nurse can have more than one uniform.)

3. Everyone's gift is on their desk.
4. It's getting dark, so we must hurry.
5. I'm not going to drive in bad weather.
6. She can't understand this simple request.
7. He hasn't called us yet.
8. Please write lowercase i's.
9. Are these 0's, o's, or 9's?
10. The printers are not working.
11. Its programs are boring.
12. These receipts are not mine, but yours.
13. We had lots of fun in the '70s.
14. The windowpane breaks if you open it forcefully.
15. Who's interested in joining the writers' club.
16. All our doctors are board-certified MDs.

15 B:

1. **He'd** love to have ice cream, too.
2. **They'll** let you know.
3. **We're** getting late for school.
4. They **aren't** working in the kitchen.
5. **They're** playing outside.
6. We **don't** want to talk now on this topic.
7. He **doesn't** follow orders.
8. She **wasn't** interested in cleaning her room.
9. It **doesn't** matter what people think.
10. **It's** been a long time since we met.
11. **They've** a good camera.
12. We **haven't** packed for the trip yet.
13. **It'd** be wonderful if you could join us.
14. **What's** the time?
15. **There's** a water fountain behind the tree.

16. Quotation Marks

16 A:

1. "Turn the volume of the TV down," shouted my sister, from her room.
2. He asked me to explain my article to him.
3. "Now," the lawyer said, "we have to think about this case in a different way."
4. "Hurry, before the sale ends!" our store is advertising.
5. The manager asked, "How many customers visited our store today?"
6. Did your teacher ask, "Why are you riding the bus today?"
7. Are you attending the cookery class "Making Birthday Cakes"?
8. Your essay, "A History of Cars," has many grammar mistakes.

9. The story "Spot Workers Who Steal" in *Life Today* magazine is interesting.
10. The boss said, "Tina wrote, 'I am resigning immediately.'"

17. Semicolon

17 A:

1. This month I will read your essays; next month I will grade them.
2. If she likes the teacher, she will continue the class; if I have the time, I will take her to class.
3. The airport security took too much time; therefore, I missed my flight.
4. They are painting my office; nevertheless, I still have to work from the office.
5. I'm flying to India; he's flying to Japan.
6. To travel abroad, you need three important things; for example, a passport, visa, and ticket are definitely needed.
7. When I visit the doctor, he answers my questions; but he does not return my phone calls.
8. For this function we are inviting Daisy, the actress; Adam, a popular model; Tanya, a TV host; and Sunny, the famous singer.
9. I saw two stray cats today; I usually notice only stray dogs every day.
10. I need these things; namely, an Internet connection, a cell phone service, cable TV, and taxi service.

18. Colon

18A:

1. The actors in the play are Mary, the mother; Anthony, the father; Daisy, the daughter; Shirin, Mary's friend; and Sunny, Shirin's husband.
2. The day-care center needs items such as bottles, diapers, tissue boxes, and snacks.
3. Dear Sir**:**
4. She made it very clear to all of us: "I'm not attending the meeting."
5. Kim traveled to Japan, Malaysia, Singapore, and India.
6. I am reading the book *Family: How to Keep the Love.*
7. The project leader started the meeting with this quote: "In order to succeed, you have to believe that you can."
8. He has to be at the office at 8:30 a.m.
9. Before we left for the trip, we checked for the following**:** passport, ticket, driver's license, medicines, laptop computer, phone, and chargers.
10. The ratio of unemployed people to employed stands at 4**:**1.

19. Hyphen

19A:

1. My babysitter loves **sun-dried** tomatoes.
2. First, we will teach you a **user-friendly** program.
3. To get a job, you must be **eighteen years old.**

4. Most of our **twelve-year-old** students are good readers.
5. A **middle-aged** man was standing at the bus stop.
6. Some people are very **narrow-minded.**
7. Sarah is a **hard-working** girl.
8. Until the **nineteen-seventies**, children spent a lot of time playing outdoors with their friends.
9. **One-fourth** of the class was absent one day before the exam.
10. We had to take the stairs from his **seventh-floor** apartment.

20. Dash

20A:

1. Preparing well for the exam—many times, but not always—helps to score well.
2. Please book a family restaurant—a quiet, nonsmoking place with a children's play area—to celebrate Sara's birthday.
3. I have ordered a long beautiful blue dress—with lace embroidery and beads—for the wedding.
4. When we were taking pictures by the Great Wall of China—oh, let me see this text message.
5. My purse that was stolen had these important items—eyeglasses, two credit cards, $500 cash, my driver's license, and my passport.
6. I would like to hire Ali as the film director—he is the best director, and he had said that he would like to work with me.
7. "Quickly take the glass bowl from his hand or—" shouted mother, but the baby threw it, and the bowl broke.

21. Parentheses

21A:

1. He brought a plant (it's poisonous) from another country.
2. If you need help, please call me on my phone (number 202-303-4004).
3. Dr. Patrick D'Souza (a family friend) is giving a lecture on depression.
4. The boy's aunt (a cruel woman) has been staying with them for years.
5. My friend Aisha Patel (do you remember her?) is migrating to the United States.

22. Brackets

22A:

1. "The leaves of this herb [coriander] are used as a garnish in Latin American, Indian, and Chinese dishes," the teacher explained.
2. "Emma finished her monthly pocket money in two days [she bought expensive clothes] and wants to borrow some from me."
3. "He [George Washington] was the first president of the United States of America."
4. "The boy's aunt is cruel [she hits and locks up the boy], so we want to make sure the boy stays only with his parents and not with the aunt."

5.   He could not go out to play [he had lot of homework], so he is very upset.

25. *Italics* and <u>Underlining</u>

25A: Underline or put in quotations the appropriate titles below.

1.   My son loves the book <u>Animal Homes</u>.
2.   <u>Voyager 2</u> is the first spacecraft to fly by the planet Uranus.
3.   The <u>Andaman Express</u>, a long-distance express train in India, runs between Chennai and Jammu.
4.   Do you have a copy of <u>Newsweek</u>?
5.   I'm reading an article titled "What We Know About the Universe." [short work]
6.   Let's watch the television show <u>America's Funniest Home Videos</u>.

■ ■ ■

Dear Learners,

Grammar is about using rules that explain how to make words work together correctly. And studying a grammar book is a big achievement, so congratulations for acquiring new knowledge and confidence in your English language skills.

Easy-to-Learn English Grammar and Punctuation is for the English learner who is curious and intelligent, not afraid to ask questions, and wonders about confusing grammar elements. Whether you study grammar from this book or any other reference book, you should be very proud of yourself that you have taken the right steps toward building and strengthening your foundation in English.

Remember, even the grammarians, English teachers and professors, writers, editors, and others who work on grammar topics every day need to check their grammar. And we all make mistakes every now and then, but we can keep improving our English by using this guide or other grammar books as a reference.

Part 2 of this book not only covers rules and explanations on advanced grammar topics but also offers interesting arguments about the tricky and varying usage of words and sentences. It also engages the learner on topics outside grammar as well and will provide answers to many of your questions that you always wanted to know. Please see page 205 for an excerpt from Part 2.

I hope you continue on your independent, mentally stimulating, and fun-filled grammar journey with Part 2. Please send any questions or suggestions you might have to the addresses below.

Congratulations and best wishes,

Sitara Maruf

Sitara Maruf, Success Time, P.O. Box 83596, Gaithersburg, MD 20883-3596, USA
E-mail: 1) info@ successtime.co   2) info@learngrammar.net
Websites: 1) www.successtime.co   2) www.learngrammar.net

■ ■ ■

Excerpt from "Nouns" Part 2

Many people argue that if *Internet* and *World Wide Web* are proper nouns, then *universe* and *sky* should be proper nouns too.

Let's consider what makes a proper noun. A proper noun is a specific name that someone gives to one particular person, place, animal, or thing that has a definite form and size, and proper nouns are capitalized. The *Internet* is the proper name given to a specific international computer network that itself connects countless other computer networks. Similarly, *World Wide Web* is a proper name given to a part of the Internet that connects documents using hyperlinks.

On the other hand, the universe is a system of matter and energy and is not considered one specific thing. The universe is a fluid phenomenon, as is air, space, sky, or water, none of which have a definite shape or size. Also, there may be many more universes. Therefore, *universe* falls in the category of common mass nouns, just like *sky, air, space,* and *water.*

A noun does not become a proper noun because of its importance to humankind, but it becomes a proper noun if you name a living or nonliving thing that has a definite form. For example, if you have the tiniest fish as a pet, and you name it Zoomy, you have to capitalize the *Z* in *Zoomy*, because you have given this name to one particular fish.

Then what about the *sun, moon,* and *earth*? Don't they have definite shapes and sizes, and they are unique to us, so why are they not considered proper nouns? Even if the *sun, moon,* and *earth* are unique to us and our solar system, they are not unique bodies in the universe. However, most of the time when we refer to the sun, moon, or earth, we are referring to *our* sun, moon, and earth. Therefore, we can write the words that refer to these celestial bodies as either proper nouns (*Sun, Moon,* and *Earth*) or common nouns (*sun, moon,* and *earth*) by applying one of these two rules:

(1) The words *Sun, Moon,* and *Earth* are proper nouns—and therefore capitalized—when we write them in an astronomical or technical context:

> ⋗ The Sun is a large ball of hot gases.
> ⋗ Our Sun is a medium-sized star and is like the billions of other stars in the universe.
> ⋗ The Moon has plains and mountains.
> ⋗ The brightest object in the night sky is the Moon.
> ⋗ The first astronauts landed on the Moon in 1969.

▷ The Earth is the third planet from the Sun.
▷ The planet Jupiter is eleven times bigger than Earth.
▷ So far, scientists know of life on only one planet: Earth.

(2) The words **sun, moon,** and **earth** written in a general way or in a plural form are common nouns and not capitalized, unless they begin a sentence.

▷ The sun was shining, so we did not feel very cold.
▷ Good and bad people live on earth.
▷ By the light of the moon, the mountaineers were able to find their way.
▷ The planet Jupiter has many moons.

■ ■ ■

About the Author

Sitara Maruf's experience includes serving as a print and broadcast journalist, a technical science writer and editor, a press officer, and an English professor in the United States.

She earned a master of arts degree in journalism and public affairs from American University in Washington, DC, and a master of science degree in biochemistry from University of Pune, India.

She has also served as a communications and media director in a governor's office. As a journalist, Sitara Maruf is credited with numerous articles, press releases, radio and television broadcasts, and interviews.

In the effort to promote English literacy among the underprivileged and those with a weak foundation in English, Sitara Maruf volunteers as an English instructor at community centers and in overseas literacy projects. She additionally teaches her original curriculum, *Easy-to-Learn English Grammar and Punctuation*, at Success Time Academy and to overseas students via videoconferencing.

Sitara Maruf lives with her husband and three children in the United States.

■ ■ ■

Made in the USA
Lexington, KY
19 September 2016